Kuntao Prodigy

Willem A. Reeders and His Elusive Martial System

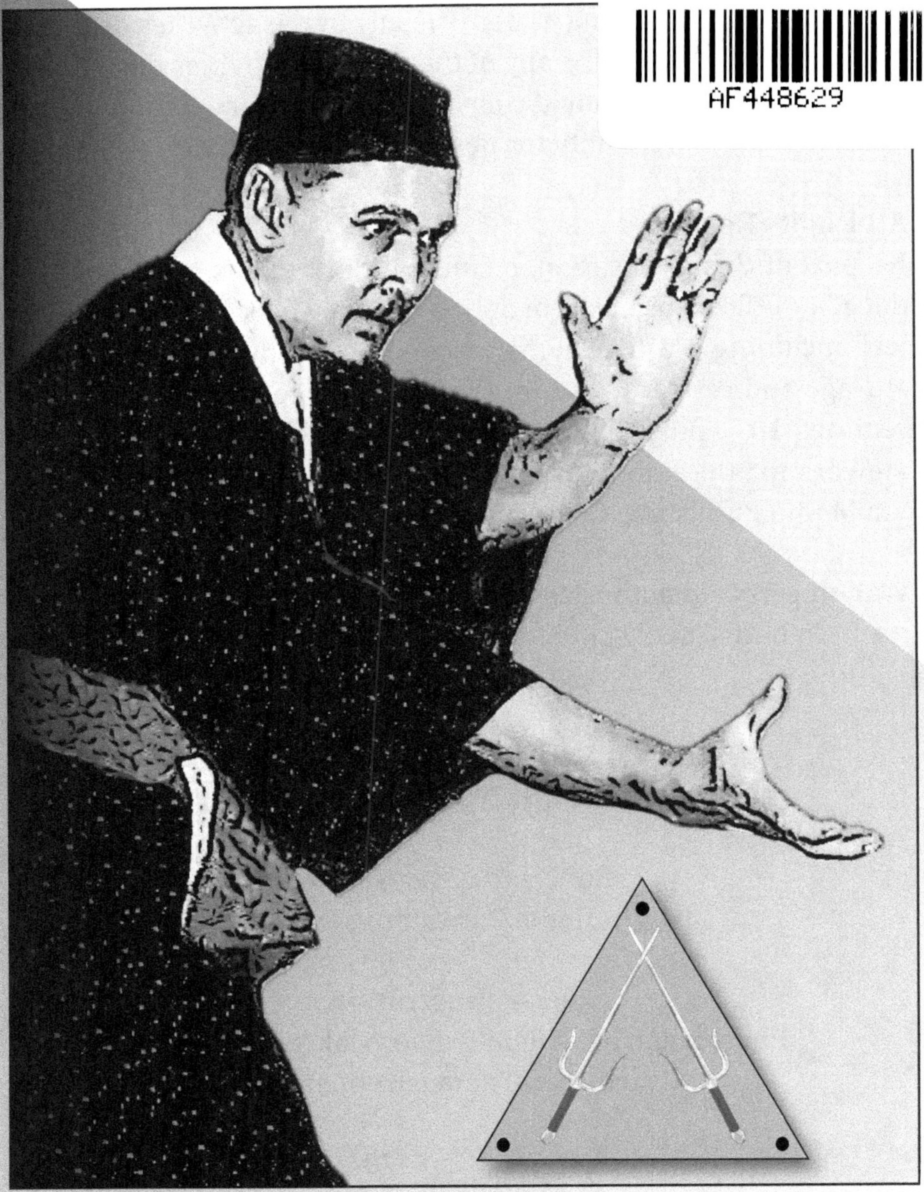

Via Media

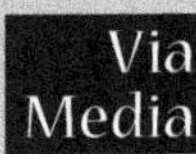

by Michael A. DeMarco, M.A.

Copyright © 2026
by Via Media Publishing Company
941 Calle Mejia #822, Santa Fe, NM 87501 USA

Book and cover design
by Via Media Publishing Company

Cover illustration
Photograph of Willem Reeders taken in Erie, PA.
Courtesy of Thomas Pepperman.

ISBN 979-8-218-79494-1

www.viamediapublishing.com

Dedication

To the memories of my kuntao mentors
for their time and effort in sharing their art:
Arthur Sykes, Thomas Pepperman, and Richard Lopez.

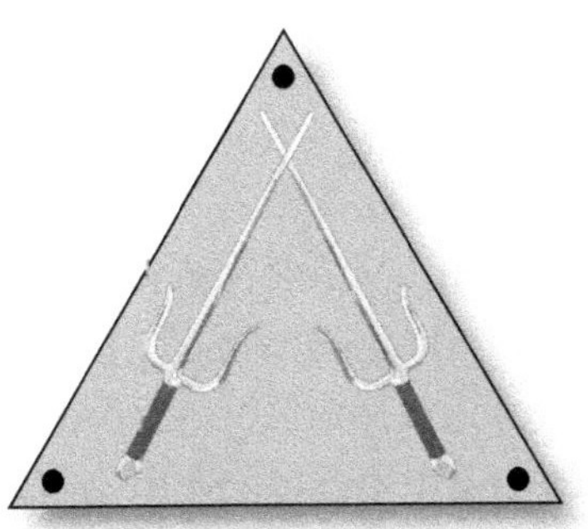

Acknowledgment

A deep bow of gratitude to the following
for their friendship, hospitality, and sharing
of their valuable time discussing the life of Willem
Reeders and his kuntao teachings: Vivianne Lauxen,
Robert Servidio, Joe Salomone, and Reginald McKissick.

Readers' Comments

"In a martial arts landscape often organized around structured systems and fixed lineages, *Kuntao Prodigy* presents a rare and nuanced account of a tradition that resists such categorization. Michael DeMarco approaches the life and work of Willem Reeders with both critical rigor and respect for the complexities of oral history, carefully navigating the tension between documented fact and enduring narrative.

What emerges is not a closed system, but an open, adaptive body of knowledge, shaped by cultural context, personal experience, and continuous transformation. Reeders' art reflects a confluence of Chinese kuntao and Indonesian silat, yet ultimately transcends stylistic boundaries. Its transmission, as the book makes clear, is necessarily fragmentary.

From my dual perspective as a long-time practitioner of pencak silat and a professional engaged in movement science and martial pedagogy, this portrayal resonates deeply. It reflects an understanding of martial knowledge as embodied, relational, and context-dependent—qualities that challenge conventional notions of standardization and replication. Rather than attempting to reconstruct a definitive system, *Kuntao Prodigy* offers a valuable and honest exploration of how martial knowledge is lived, transmitted, and inevitably reshaped over time. In doing so, it contributes meaningfully to both the practice and the study of martial arts."

> ➥ **Jan Bloem**, Drs., State University of Groningen
> Founder of D.A.T. Movement and member
> of the Dutch Pencak Silat Federation

"Many thanks to Michael DeMarco for offering a well-researched publication on the life of master warrior Willem Reeders. The time and savvy required to produce this book is appreciated.

In the early 1960s, Erie Pennsylvania was a hotbed of martial arts—the time in which Reeders made his USA appearance. His presence and fighting skills shattered the common view of what martial arts fully entail, enlightening his followers. Now we have this book, *Kuntao Prodigy*, kicking open a door allowing a bright light to shine on his system. After our decades of study and friendship, Reeders remained an enigmatic individual whose martial proficiency was beyond doubt."

➡ **Robert Servidio,** Grandmaster
Willem Reeders' Kuntao System

"As President of the Dutch Pencak Silat Federation (including Kuntao), I'm always thrilled when new books about Southeast Asian martial arts are published.

In *Kuntao Prodigy*, the author not only captures key values of the art but also provides a comprehensive overview of its evolution over a specific timeframe. My experience within the international silat community has rarely led me to a work that so effectively bridges tradition historical facts and modern application.

The book delves deeply into aspects I've personally encountered during my active training with individuals connected to Mr. Reeders and those mentioned in the book. It's a must-read for anyone interested in Pencak Silat–Kuntao, particularly those who appreciate its background and origins."

➡ **Olivier Blanquet**, President
Netherlands Pencak Silat Federation

"Thank you so much for writing a book about my grandfather, Willem Reeders. *Kuntao Prodigy* provides factual information and photographs meaningful for our family and the Reeders martial lineage. I heard stories about him from my grandmother Marcella. At her request, I went to the bridge over the river Kwai when I travelled to Thailand. I got a glimpse about the conditions in the POW camps and it made me cry. My grandfather died on my birthday, August 14. So he will always be connected to me in that special way. I hope everybody will love reading this book as much as I did."

➡ **Vivianne Lauxen**, M.Ed., Utrecht University
Willem Reeders' granddaughter

Grandmaster
Willem Reeders
廖崇
photo courtesy of Robert Servidio

TABLE OF CONTENTS

Bromo Volcano • East Java, Indonesia
ID 31875023 © Noppakun | Dreamstime.com

Preface

Of the small group of kuntao teachers that arrived from Southeast Asia to teach in the United States, most would agree Willem Reeders (1917–1990) was the most gifted. His first-generation students were fortuitous and thanked their fateful stars for his instruction. Most of these students have now passed and they've expressed their thankfulness even in their obituaries.

Today, Reeders' kuntao is being taught and practiced by second and third generation offspring. Although none fully embody the knowledge and skills of the grandmaster, together they reflect parts of his image and many segments of his martial repertoire. Thus, some call his teaching the "broken mirror system," knowing his students and descendants could only absorb fragments of his complete system.

For those trying to carry on his tradition—and for others who just have a passing interest in Reeders' history and fighting art—there is a void of material to draw upon: few writings, articles, books, photographs, films or videos. Inquisitive minds resort to informal discussions with first generation students, especially those who have spent the most time studying with Reeders.

After looking over all the information obtained about Reeders, his kuntao and leading disciples, we find an array of stories, some based on solid facts and other are laced with exaggeration, aggrandizement, and unsubstantiated claims. How are we to separate the wheat from the chaff?

The oral tradition surrounding Reeders—the one we've heard and read about over the decades—has largely become accepted because early narratives have been repeated, expanded upon, and spread. I was introduced to kuntao and Art Sykes by my friend

JAVA

Drawn and engraved by
Jan van Braam and
Gerard onder de Linden.

NLB Singapore,
David Parry Southeast
Asian Map Collection.
CC0 1.0 Universal

Thomas Pepperman in 1965. Sykes was one of Reeders' most dedicated first-generation students as Pepperman was of Sykes. Since those early days I could not believe nor disbelieve all the remarkable stories I heard about Grandmaster Reeders. I simply acknowledged that I didn't know for sure what was true, partially true, or false.

A few years ago, I put a few photos of Reeders on my Facebook page. I read one comment: "That's my grandpa!" . . . I was shocked to find out that Reeders' granddaughter had written from the Netherlands. We started communicating. I sent her a full-page summary of stories I heard about the grandmaster: royal Dutch and Chinese ancestry, family plantation in Indonesia, World War II stories of espionage, etc. I asked if she could verify any of the questions posed. "Yes! All true!" she replied.

Reeders' relatives in the Netherlands heard the same accounts of his life that we received here in the United States. It turns out that they, like us, only had rumors to ruminate on. So, our collective stories agree but remain unverified. This little book attempts to bring at least some solid facts to supplement the legend.

In chapter one, a coverage of the historical setting is provided as a background of someone of Dutch heritage growing up in Indonesia at the start of the 20th century to the end of World War II. These years coincide with Reeders' early family life, his service in the war, the end of Dutch rule in Indonesia, and Reeders' eventual departure to the West.

Chapter two is a review of what has been generally accepted as the history of Willem Reeders, his ancestry and teachings. Many will

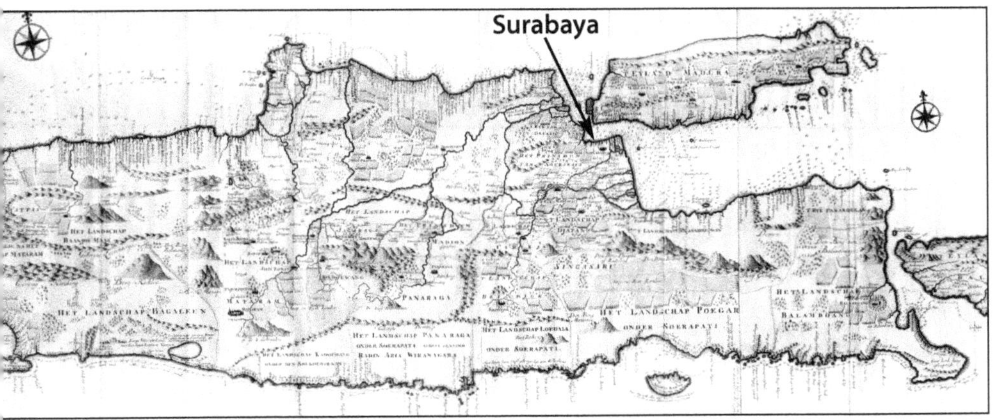

be familiar with the material covered here. Much has been copied, repeated, and repeated in discussions and on internet chat. Little is mentioned in this book about his family or his students. The purpose here is to focus on the man and his martial art.

The content in the following chapter comes from a different approach. It utilizes academic standards of research to reach solid conclusions about what we can know as fact, or it forces us to conclude that some inquires reach a dead end, producing no confirmation.

Some say we cannot rely on websites like Ancestry.com, but apparently, they have not learned how it works as a research tool. Each name on an ancestral chart has meaning derived only by supporting documentation: birth, marriage, divorce, photographs, census records, travel documents, passenger lists, obituaries, military records, newspapers, maps, and more. Combine this type of research utilizing respected publications and online sources, and a new picture emerges. This book contains documentation that has previously been overlooked.

An analysis of chapters one, two and three is provided in chapter four. The Reeders' story has been obscured by his own actions, and those of his students and others. The human condition has played a role: ego, promotion, misunderstandings, exaggerations, etc. So Reeders' story also provides insights for understanding the lives and practices of other leading martial artists.

Chapter five provides an overview of the theory and practices of Reeders' kuntao system. His theory was based on practicality stemming from Indonesian warrior traditions and social conflicts occurring during his time. All else he considered fluff. His technical repertoire was eclectic. If a highly skilled martial art master could put his or her knowledge in one book, Reeders would need a facility such as the Library of Congress. There are musicians, linguists, and others who appear "once in a hundred years." Reeders is in this category, so we can only provide an overview of his system in this book.

An appendix highlights some of the hurdles regarding communicating without a fluent grasp of foreign languages. When Reeders arrived in America, he did not speak English very well and students may not have clearly understood what he wanted to convey. Also, most Americans were unfamiliar with Asian languages, history, and culture, including martial arts terminology. Proper communication can only be done when the terminology and associated meanings are clearly defined. Otherwise, as the Greeks say: "It's all Chinese to me!"

This little book is a humble contribution to kindred kuntao practitioners. I've tried to provide an additional way to view Willem Reeders as a person, even though his kuntao will remain largely ineffable. Of course, I hope readers will appreciate the new details provided here. Others will reject some information in this book—not because of possible poor research or faulty logic on my part—but simply because they wish to ignore it. However, the material will certainly arouse curiosity and stimulate thought.

Above all, I recognize Willem Reeders as a martial art prodigy. He had a rare natural ability to absorb and embody any martial art he had opportunity to see. He also lived and survived through difficult times in both Indonesia and America. This greatly affected his personality and relationships with his family and students. It is up to us to go on from here. Kuntao practitioners are responsible for their use of the art and how they may teach. Personal character and martial art skills can be developed and polished together. Kuntao, as one of the most lethal martial arts, certainly needs tempering by good character.

Michael A. DeMarco

Santa Fe, New Mexico, 17 April 2026

chapter I

Life in Dutch-Indonesia

Strangers Knocking

What was it like in Java, Indonesia, when a Dutch infant named Willem Reeders entered the world on 29 October 1917? Just by blood, he was privileged by being a European in a land with over 1,300 ethnic groups. The largest ethnic group in Indonesia is the Javanese. They've been here over a million years with ancestors migrating out of Africa. Since then, Indonesia came to be populated by waves of peoples from near and far shores adding to the native population. To understand Java at the start of the twentieth century, we can look at the most important groups who relocated to the island.

Migrations came from Indochina before 3,000 BCE and a thousand years later others came from Taiwan. Traders from India and China arrived in large numbers starting in the first century CE having an enormous cultural impact. Another infusion came with the Arabs and Persians (c. 9th-13th centuries CE). Over the centuries, the spread of Islam eventually turned Indonesia into the largest Muslim country in the world.

Among Europeans, the Portuguese were the first to arrive, reaching the Malaccas, often called the "Spice Islands," by 1512. They conquered Malacca with about 1,200 men and seventeen ships. Spanish ships soon followed to compete over who would control the clove and nutmeg trade. The British established a trade and briefly controlled Java.

The Dutch landed in western Java in 1596. Seeking to dominate the spice trade in the region, they established the Dutch East India

The Return to Amsterdam of the Second Expedition to the East Indies.
Signed oil painting by Hendrick Cornelisz Vroom, 1599. Rijksmuseum.

Inset: The Arms of the Dutch East India Company by Jeronimus Becx (II), 1651. From the collection of the Rijksmuseum in Amsterdam.

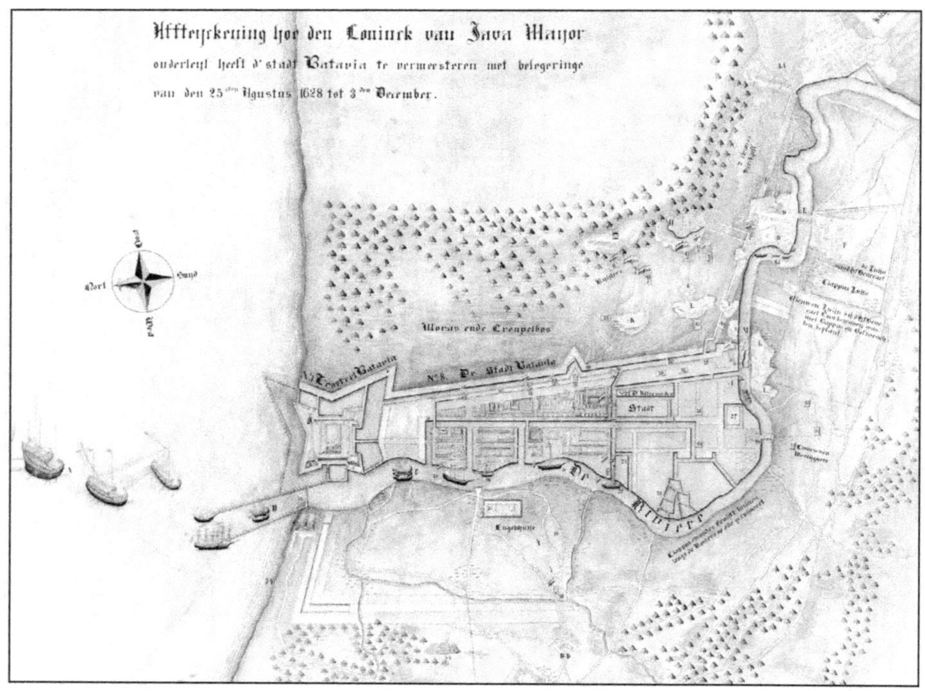

Above: 1628 map of the colonial Dutch occupation of Batavia (Jakarta), Indonesia. *ID 160089388 © Dennis Van De Water | Dreamstime.com*

Below: Aerial view of a pentagonal fort built by Dutch in the Banda Neira Island, Maluku, Indonesia. *ID 125521303 © Bidouze Stephane | Dreamstime.com*

Company in 1602. Many employees were German. Headquartered in Batavia, now known as Jakarta, the company is noted as being the world's first multinational corporation. Its powers were beyond what we usually think of as a business corporation, acting much like a government with the authority to construct fortresses, wage war, and negotiate treaties. Their influence was backed by a private army and a massive fleet. Meanwhile, the relationship among regional Indonesian rulers was characterized by "assassinations, coups and failed military adventures (Recklifs, 1993:33). The 17th century was much of the same. The Dutch had to constantly struggle to hold their position amid other political and military groups. The following century provides more details, illustrating the growing complexity of the multifaceted Dutch-Indonesia.

By the 18th century, many Indonesian cities, particularly along the coastlines, were populated by a mix of people from ancient and more recent immigrations. These were Chinese, Arab, Southeast Asians, and European settlers. Associated with the spice trade and plantations, we also find many enslaved people were brought in from other regions to work the fields. Striving to improve their own standards of living, the various political and social groups were fated to be in constant contention over commercial interests.

Almost all from the Netherlands who came to Indonesia were involved with the Dutch East India Company. The abbreviation for the company is VOC, derived from the Dutch name (*Vereenigde Oostindische Compagnie*). Commonly referred to as VOC, the company was present in Indonesia from 1602 to 1800. After its formal closure, the Dutch government took over, placing the land under colonial rule until 1949.

We may imagine VOC being run as a modern company, but the administrative personnel and the common employee proved to possess their own unique attributes. The early adventures who set out to Indonesia for trade set the standard. Scholar M.C. Ricklefs wrote of the first Portuguese settling in Indonesia: "This outpost at the other end of the earth rarely attracted any but the most desperate and avaricious" (1993:24). Their presence in Malacca caused "disruption and disorganization of the trade network" (Ricklefs, 1993:26). Of the Dutch, many employees were "adventurers, vagabonds, criminals, and the unfortunate from throughout Europe," "inefficiency, dishonesty, nepotism and alcoholism were widespread in the VOC" (Ricklefs, 1993:27).

From the short summary above, it is apparent that the Indonesian lands were under immense stress for hundreds of years. In the numerous kingdoms, sultanates, and regions people engaged others of strange nationalities, languages, social-economic classes, religious beliefs, political views—each group seeking peace, profit, and stability for themselves. A common thread throughout these centuries was conflict. From tribal warfare to international incidents, martial skills were valued as necessary for self-protection from the dangers of a violent social-political atmosphere. It can be said that one lived on a wing and a prayer.

Men in a trance with a kris and barong.
ID 51768698 © Rahmat Nugroho | Dreamstime.com

Chasing the Magic

Very ancient animistic beliefs are embedded in the soul of native Indonesian religions. There are invisible spirits present in all things, from rocks, rivers and trees to the weather, volcanos and people. Mediums communicate with spirits of the dead. Mystical experience was sought to establish a union with ultimate reality, which often is named God or the Divine. When petitioned properly, forces of the unseen world will aid the living.

Over centuries, these vital elements from the native religion fused with other spiritual traditions. The syncretism naturally took on different expressions by people, creating a rich variety of beliefs and practices. The officially recognized religions in Indonesia are Islam, Protestantism, Catholicism, Hinduism, Buddhism, and Confucianism. However, there remains a ubiquitous presence of the ancient beliefs which Indonesians refer to as the "flow of belief" (*aliran kepercayaan*).

In premodern Indonesia, headhunting had been part of warfare. It was believed that through ending an enemy's life, the victor would capture his enemy's warrior spirit and bring additional power and prestige to himself. This ancient warrior tradition developed in different ways over the following centuries, still seeking ways to empower the warrior.

When Islam, Hinduism and Buddhism entered the Indonesian archipelago, mystical elements played largely in conversions to the religions. Religious and secular literature are peppered with stories of magical events. Visual and performing arts often include sacred elements of a fantastic nature. Gamelan orchestral music is quite hypnotic, sounding as if created by supernatural forces. Puppets, kris knives, batik fabrics and specific dances "had spiritual personalities and released supernatural energies… Elaborate rituals and rules therefore surrounded the arts of Indonesia (Ricklefs, 1993:57).

Texts, inscriptions, and myths ascribed to the supernatural were used to foretell the future. Here is an example. After a long period of rule, one kingdom remained prosperous and strong, able to defeat any invader. However, the king believed strongly in the spiritual ebb and flow of set cycles. When attacked by another kingdom, he simply submitted to the will of his gods. It was the end of a predicted dynastic cycle, so the king accepted his fate. The unseen forces played heavily on political powers. "A sense of legitimacy, with its supernatural sanctions, was one of the prime pillars of kingship" (Ricklefs, 1993:99). Local and regional rulers had their stock of holy regalia (*pusaka*), symbolizing their supernatural support. One example of this is the case of Pangeran Dipanagara (1785–1855). He was famed for having numerous religious visions as proof of his divinely appointed position as a future king of Java. What could be better than this five star review?

A newer school of thought started in the United States and took hold in Central Java in the 1880s called Theosophy. Its unique blend of the old mystical traditions with other Eastern and Western philosophies presented teachings on the divine, cosmos, and humanity. It appealed to the Javanese elites to foster the concept of national identity.

The use of amulets, sacred syllables and prayers are utilized throughout Southeast Asia by martial artists as ways to assist, protect, and provide special physical and energetic powers. Floor patterns are inscribed for practitioners to learn footwork, mark cosmic geometry, and define energetic defensive barriers. Psychic power is certainly a draw for studying martial arts. Superheroes rely on superpowers. In a land of physical confrontations, it was natural for martial artists to chase the magic.

The metal gongs are called *talempong* and the flat drum is called an *adok*.

The ensemble includes two *gendang* drums and two hand-held *talempong* gongs. These two drums have been passed down for fourteen generations and are said to house spirits.

Left: The silat practitioner on the right is using a dynamic crane stance (*tagak itiak*) as a transition into a retreating movement to evade the anticipated kick from his opponent. (Style: Silek Bungo)

Left: The silat practitioner on the right is retreating into a crane stance (*pitunggua*) as a defense against a leg sweep. (Style: Silek Kumango).

Photographs on pages 10 and 11 courtesy of Dr. Kirstin Pauka.

Life Expectancy

Willem Reeders and his siblings were born in Surabaya, in northeast Java. Their parents were married in Probolinggo, about sixty-six miles (107km) further east. Living in proximity to the major port city, it seems they would have been exposed for many years to the complex social conditions of the early twentieth century.

Surabaya was already a bustling Islamic port in the early sixteenth century. By the following century it was a leading coastal power. In 1620, the Dutch describe the port city as being built on the coast of the Java Sea, expanding about twenty-three miles (37km) in circumference. This was surrounded by a canal, and the city was protected with cannons. Surabaya was a financial trade center and a military base.

Sultan Agung (r. 1613–46), king of Mataram in central Java, has been described as the "greatest of Java's warriors." He conquered Surabaya in 1625, mainly by destroying the rice fields and starving the city population. Another famous Indonesian warrior of the seventeenth century was prince Arung Palakka. This rebel and his band settled in Batavia (Jakarta) and joined the VOC as soldiers, greatly impressing the Dutch with their martial skills. With their assistance, they proved their worth in Dutch conflicts.

Over the centuries, Surabaya and northeast Java faced many of the same problems, such as major warfare with regional groups. The Dutch East India Company's base in Surabaya was always unstable with risks from every quarter. When European and Asian foreigners arrived looking for work, some couldn't find any employment. An option would be to join criminal gangs. Brigands roamed the land, robbing and looting when opportunity arose. Rebellions were regular. When Mount Merapi erupted in 1822, it was taken as an omen of impeding chaos. Omen or not, it was easy to predict that chaos would follow chaos. The Dutch had to keep constant vigilance.

Warfare was the major destructive force. Small skirmishes were regular. Major engagements with large military forces lead to massive losses among soldiers and civilian populations. The disruption of agriculture lead to sickness, dysentery, and starvation. Epidemics, such as cholera, hit the population sporadically. Natural disasters too often accompanied man-made disasters.

The violent times paralleled political dealings. Political intrigue came in every fashion. Plots, rumors, alliances, and assassinations were part of governing. Even marriage diplomacy was tried, without satisfactory results. The widespread use of opium in Java only gave temporary peace. Its daily used by hundreds of thousands of people did provide a substantial revenue source for the Dutch colonial state.

How could rebellions, massacres and warfare be part of normal life during the time of Dutch presence in Indonesia? Ongoing conflicts were considered normal, as between religious ideologies, political outlooks, military strategies, and economic competition. The Dutch were considered as a leading political presence mainly because they had formidable military power. However, their leadership was far from satisfactory, with economic losses for the company and the Netherlands as well as for Indonesians.

The VOC had a reputation. The heads of the Dutch East India Company (VOC) in Asia were known as Governor-Generals. It seems most of them were role models of debauchery and alcoholism. Some embezzled large sums from their plantations and trade negotiations. The result was inefficiency in their work and duties. Their failures led to brutality towards the Indonesians. Hatred among numerous groups fueled further frustrations and conflicts. As Ricklefs writes (1993:82): "VOC personnel also had little reason to think that they found themselves in a tropical paradise. If they were not killed in a brutal war or a local quarrel, they faced the near-certainty of an early death from disease or alcoholism."

When VOC formally dissolved in 1800, Indonesia came under direct Dutch colonial rule for nearly 150 more years. Any major events in Indonesia would affect the Netherlands, and vice versa. For instance, the Napolean wars affected life in Indonesia. World Wars I and II stand out since they colored Willem Reeders' years from his birth until he emigrated to North America.

Dutch Colonial Period

As could be expected, the colonial rule allowed corruption and abuse to continue. The aristocrats continued to enjoy their privileges while Indonesians experienced great suffering. The situation was exasperated by rapid population growth, almost tripling in Java from 1830 to 1890, going from 7 million to over 23.6 million.

Reeders was living in Java. This island and neighboring Madura held 70 percent of the Indonesian population. According to early records, the European population in Java was only 17,285 in 1852, but in 1900 it increased to 62,447. By1920, the overall population of Java and Madura reached 34.4 million. With the vast majority living in horrid conditions, the population had only 667 doctors. Within Indonesia, an institute for university-level education did not exist until 1920. Exports fell and prices fluctuated for the major products of coffee, sugar and indigo. Financial crises hit the Netherland and Indonesia, making life more intolerable in Java.

Entering the 20th century, a variety of ideas and methods were presented as possible solutions for the existing social-political problems. Military might pressed on while alternatives were being considered. Old and modern political parties contended as did private organizations. Many sought inspiration in messianic ideas, particularly from Islamic and native traditions.

Greater concern for the lives of common people started to be expressed. Welfare programs came into being and trade unions formed to protect workers.

Actions by the Dutch also reflect a greater concern for the native population. What became known as the Ethical Policy developed in part from as realization that the Netherlands owed Indonesia a huge debt for the centuries of exploitation. Dutch rule had negative and positive impacts. "Feudal political systems, slavery, widow-burning, internecine wars, head-hunting, cannibalism, piracy and other unacceptable practices were being abolished under Dutch rule" (Ricklefs, 1993:146). Advances were made in the education field, including acceptance of women into the system. Agriculture was improved with better irrigation systems and seed selections. However, all the advances could not keep up with the population boom. An answer for this was to focus on emigration.

Search for a National identity

During the first quarter of the 20th century, the multi-layered fabric of Indonesian society posed a question on how to unite all in the islands with a revived national identity. One plan was to arrange for Indonesian autonomy within a Dutch-Indonesian union, but there was also a growing belief that an independent Indonesian state could be established. A flourishing number of newspapers and literary works focused on these topics.

Progress was slowly being made in the political and economic areas. A booming interest in the automobile industry brought about a need for rubber and oil, which became big export products for Indonesia. Japan was a major importer. Japanese interest grew and their presence in Indonesia increased during the 1920s. As they developed their businesses, they conducted intelligence activities and sought to raise pro-Asian sentiment. They hoped to sway the Indonesians and other Asia countries to fall under a Japanese dominated region of control. Many were attracted to their anti-Western propaganda.

Japanese influence was on the rise while Europe was absorbed in World War One (1914–1918). The war disrupted European communications with Asian areas, including shipping and imports. The Netherlands and other European countries redirected funds into their military objectives and cut money from projects in Indonesia, including the much-needed welfare activities.

The world was witnessing the rise of fascism in Europe and Japan. Aware of Japan's interest in Indonesia, especially as oil was necessary for their military to function, exports to Japan from Indonesia were halted in 1941. Japanese assets were frozen. These actions made Japan more aggressive. In the following year, they destroyed the Dutch colonial state, making it impossible for the Dutch to cooperated with the Indonesians in any way.

When Japan attacked Pearl Harbor on 7 December 1941, they became involved in World War Two. Just over a month later, they invaded Indonesia. The Dutch in Indonesia were forced to surrender to Japan in March 1942. Java came under the Japanese 16th Army. Nearly all the Europeans were interned, which numbered about 170,000. Almost a third of these were Dutch military. Life in Indonesia was extremely difficult with shortages of food and sickness. Life in prisoner of war camps was more so. "The highest death toll was in the male civilian camps, where 40 per cent died" (Recklefs, 1993:200). Internees were forced to labor on civil and military projects as far away as Burma and Siam, today known as Myanmar and Thailand.

Japanese rule in Indonesia was more oppressive than any other colonial period. The local population stagnated for the first time in two hundred years. The Dutch and English languages were forbidden to be used and books in those languages were banned. All propaganda was made to focus on the Japanese becoming the leading Asian political and military power.

There was one person who became the most influential Indonesian during the Dutch colonial period and Japanese occupation. He was Koesno Sosrodihardjo (1901–1970), known as Sukarno. As a young man, he studied in Surabaya at a middle-school and he worked as a railway clerk. Sukarno's character made him a natural leader, and he came to play a major role in Indonesia's nationalist movement. Just his personal appearance would calm violence among relatively small local conflicts.

The Japanese invited Sukarno to Japan where he first saw a modernized country that had been industrialized. However, Sukarno's contacts with the Japanese soon changed as atomic bombs dropped on Hiroshima and later Nagasaki. Plus, the Soviet Union declared war on Japan. When Japan surrendered on 15 August 1945, Sukarno declared Indonesian independence just two days later and he became the first President of Indonesia.

Indonesian War of Independence. Dutch attack in Lombok, 1894.
J. Hoynck van Papendrecht (1858-1933).

The road to full independence for Indonesia was not totally complete. Many of the problems that existed during the Dutch periods were still of great concern, even basic needs of the population. Sukarno's government faced rebellions from several factions. Those who collaborated with the Japanese were subdued. The Dutch were trying once again to reestablish a colonial regime and the British moved into the islands of Java and Sumatra. One job the British had was to evacuate Europeans and Indo-European internees from the Japanese prisoner of war camps, including a camp in central Java called Ambarawa.

The main battle of the Indonesian Revolution took place in Surabaya. Sukarno's military was pitted against Japanese, Dutch, British and regional forces. One of the regional rebellions was led by S.M. Kartosuwirjo (1905–1962). Although his devoted followers believed he had supernatural powers, he eventually submitted to Sukarno.

The Dutch thought that their centuries-long history in Indonesia gave them the right to reestablish a colonial regime. However, the United States and allies of Australia and Britain didn't agree. American Congress threated to stop economic aid to the Netherlands, which was trying to rebuild following World War II. The Dutch had also lost all Indonesian political support. In the end, the Dutch had to give up the towns they controlled in Java and Sumatra.

Following World War II and the revolutionary period, international pressures and lengthy negotiations led to the formal establishment of the Republic of the United States of Indonesia on 27 December 1949 when the Netherlands formally transferred sovereignty to Indonesia. The newly formed republic established its constitution and government immediately after the 1945 proclamation, which served as the foundation for the state despite the ongoing internal conflicts.

Major issues remained.

Willem Reeders in the jungle on Java. Courtesy of R. Lopez.

chapter II

One Thing Leads to Another

When Willem Reeders moved to the United States and began teaching martial arts, he entered a society ripe and ready for his teachings. The country was at war. The populous was combative among themselves, largely heated by racial frictions. Even grade school children were drilled to crouch under their desks in threat of a nuclear attack. Under these tensions, people were searching for stability, safety, and peace. Many found solace by studying self-defense.

The violence and chaos of the 1960s found expression in many ways. Assassinations marked the decade with the snuffing out of lights like John Kennedy, Robert Kennedy, Malcom X, and Martin Luther King. The Vietnam War dominated the news while other warring areas ignited in the Middle East, the Sino-Indian War, the Indo-Pakistani War, and several countries were fighting for independence in Africa. Closer to home in the USA came the Cuban Missile Crisis. Racial tensions were ubiquitous with the Watts riots being only one instance. Prejudice, police brutality, and economic inequality lead to bursts of hundreds of protests.

People seeking peace in their lives found inspiration from those who worked to resolve the troubling issues of the day. One example would be Martin Luther King who delivered his "I Have a Dream" speech and later received a Nobel Peace Prize. The Apollo 11 Lunar Module Eagle landed on moon where Neil Armstrong left the first human footprints on its surface. Other notables made their impact and the future looked promising. These figureheads were supported by a massive base with high ideals. The "hippie movement" spread across the states and abroad. The Woodstock Music and Art Fair of 1969 was a highlight where musical groups spread the vibes of peace and harmony.

Martial arts practice provided an outlet for inner frustrations by punching and kicking bags, controlled sparring, and sweating. The skills learned provided a sense of self-security and protection against potential dangers on the street. Within the schools, practitioners became a "martial family," bonding with common goals. The instructor, perhaps one with solid experience, was often held in awe. A good number of the teachers were men who returned from military duties in Asia. Donn Draeger, Chuck Norris, Robert W. Smith, Frederick Peterson, and others of lesser-known names imported the arts. They had been exposed to martial styles mainly in Korea and Japan. As a result, during the late 1950s and 1960s, Americans gradually became aware of judo and karate.

In these early years, it was difficult to find a martial art teacher in the United States. Most Americans were familiar with Western style boxing and basic street fighting skills, but the "Oriental martial arts" remained a mystery. Books available about martial traditions were few and of poor quality. The internet didn't exist. No YouTube videos. No easy way to discover foreign martial styles. Few people had a concept of how many combat arts existed in Asia.

The first glimpses of the fighting techniques of karate and judo left Western observers mesmerized. Upon first exposure, the skills of a competent teacher seemed magical. They could break boards and bricks and throw attackers with techniques that seemed humanly impossible.

When Bruce Lee appeared in the TV series The Green Hornet (1966–1967), Americans began to take notice of Chinese traditions. He didn't become an international superstar until the early 1970s. A door opened with a realization that perhaps numerous centuries-old styles developed in many native cultures?

The early instructors who began teaching Asian martial art styles in America may have had a good general grasp of their arts. However, nearly one hundred percent were totally unfamiliar with the areas from which the arts derived. They didn't know the language, history or social etiquette of Asian cultures.

When Willem Reeders was discovered living in western New

York, he attracted local students such as Gary Galvin, and brothers Tom and Jerry Bradigan. A dedicated student base from Erie, Pennsylvania, regularly went to his classes. These included Robert Servidio, Artis Simmons, Arthur Sykes, Gerald Durant, Richard Lopez, Ramond Cunningham, and Tom Handest. These men were martial artists with some previous experience in both judo and karate. When their teacher Sandy Scotch moved from Erie to California in 1960, they gravitated to Reeders.

Almost all of what we learn of Reeders' life and teachings came through his first-generation students. His students arrived with the idea that they could improve their karate and judo. Richard Lopez, who studied judo in Erie and in Germany, heard Reeders was a judo master. He had many classes and memories of rough and tumble judo with Reeders, with Lopez taking the beatings. In time, he and others learned Reeders had profound skills in yet another martial art. The following pages detail what they learned of the master and of his skills.

Reeders kneeling on left with Gerald Durant. Back row, left to right: Artis Simmons, Arthur Sykes, George Carter, Richard Lopez.

Willem Reeders in a formal posture (left) and with senior students Richard Lopez (center) and Arthur Sykes (right).

Family with Royal Lines

Reeders informed his students that he taught kuntao, a family style passed on to him from his uncle. This was no regular family. Reeders was born in Indonesia of royal Dutch and Chinese blood. His grandfather Karl Lodewygk was of Dutch royalty who went to China as an emissary with the objective to establish a tea trade agreement. In Beijing, he met with the emperor and other high officials.

Karl Lodewygk was the nephew of Willem the Fifth, King of the Netherlands. Plus, Karl had marriage ties to the Earl of the House of Wieling in England. Of course, since Karl was of royal lineage he would rub elbows with Chinese royal families. He met a princess named Hap Kiem whose mother was from a southern Chinese royal family with the surname Liu. Some say Lodewygk fell in love with Hap Kiem, but it's more likely he wanted to establish a business arrangement through marriage.

Hap Kiem's younger brother, Liu Seong, liked the nobleman from Holland and tried to convince the family heads to agree to a marriage. They didn't budge and forbade a marriage. Liu Seong found a solution by arranging for Karl and Hap Kiem to secretly leave China and move to Indonesia. When the royal heads learned of the plot, they set out to arrest Liu Seong.

Guessing there would be a reprisal, Liu Seong followed the couple. He left China from a place noted as "Hekao," which may be the Hakka dialect pronunciation for the former Portuguese colony of Macao. The Chinese characters for the location could not be found, so it is impossible at this time to pinpoint the true birth home of the Liu family. Liu Seong then settled with the newlyweds on a plantation they established in Java with funds from their families. It was called the Wieling Family Plantation.

Hap Kiem and Karl had a daughter named Christina who was born in 1910. Some say Liu Seong was her brother, which shows a disagreement among the Americans on the exact relationships. Regardless, it is noted that when Christina came of age, she married Cornelis Reeders, a civil engineer living in Eastern Java. For the elaborate wedding held on the Wieling Estate, Christina wore a dress worth thousands as she mingled among one-thousand guests.

Christina and Cornelis' first offspring was a girl named Adriana Engelina born in 1914. Her brother Theo Cornelis arrived in 1920. Willem was the second offspring, born in 1917. How did he learn martial arts? What styles did he practice and with whom?

Royal Martial Arts

A key to understanding Willem Reeders martial art is linked to his uncle, Liu Seong, a Shaolin priest and a martial art master. In China, there is a history of a Southern Shaolin Temple in Fujian Province which was destroyed in the early 18th century by Qing Dynasty troops with only five monks escaping. One of these monks was related to Liu Seong. So, Liu Seong inherited martial traditions from his own royal family system as evolved from Southern Shaolin.

The Chinese who emigrated to Indonesia would often hire a martial art master to train selected family members and employees to defend their property and goods. In this case, the Wieling Plantation had a top family member become the guardian: Liu Seong. Of royal lineage and an anointed Shaolin priest, he didn't have an offspring of his own to teach as dictated according to tradition. So, little Willem Reeders, the eldest son in the royal Liu family line, was chosen to inherit the family art. A branch of the Liu Seong style is said to have been taught to the emperor's elite guards.

Willem was only four years old when Liu Seong started teaching him. His uncle was about eighty years old at that time, instructing regularly under an intense regimen. When Reeders was twelve years old, he and his uncle began a yearly trek to the northern Shaolin

Willem with his uncle. Photos courtesy of R. Lopez.

Temple in Henan Province for one-hundred days of training in martial arts, and the study of Chinese traditional medicine, philosophy, and other topics. This annual training continued for ten years, ending when Willem turned twenty-one. Thus, they became very familiar with northern Shaolin's martial systems.

In his early years, Willem attended a private Dutch-run school. Being of Dutch-Chinese blood, young Willem became a target as a foreign looking kid among the native Indonesians. Often, he'd return home from school, marked by his fights with other school children. His sister would patch ripped shirts and pants with her sewing skills.

There are many stories about Reeders skirmishing with schoolmates and others as a young adult. Another example involves a fighter known for using an axe as his weapon of choice. This man was belittling Liu Seong in conversations. Willem heard about this and confronted him, leading to a fight between axe and *taichu* (Jap. *sai*)—the latter being Reeders' favorite weapon. After a few exchanges, Willem side-slipped an axe attack, simultaneously hitting his opponent in the neck with a taichu to end the fight. In later years recounting this event, Willem told his students that it is foolish to

Left to right: Ernst de Vries, Liu Siong, and Willem Reeders in Java. 1933.

engage anyone over such idle gossip. Sometime between the ages of 21 and 25, Willem is said to have obtained a civil engineering degree. There are no stories about him being picked on during his college years.

Of course, Liu Seong had his share of combative encounters. Some wrote that Liu Seong lost his vision while still living in China when assailants threw powdered glass in his eyes. This was given as the main reason why he moved to Indonesia, avoiding any more potential challenges. It seems more logical that this attack happened in Indonesia, perhaps by two silat assassins.

Richard Lopez gives an alternate account, stating that two Japanese learned about Liu Seong's prowess. They knew if they challenged him, they would lose in any fair fight. They had a scheme. One approached Liu Seong asking if he had matches to light a cigarette. While Liu Seong was reaching into his pocket for matches, the other assailant threw powdered glass into Liu Seong's eyes that he had concealed in a handkerchief. The cutting glass didn't distract Liu Seong from matters at hand. Both assailants were killed within seconds right on the spot.

It was common in Indonesia that martial artists would make challenges, even death matches. They would sign a document in case of death to arrange for their own burial in case defeated. A blanket was placed on the ground displaying a variety of weapons. The challenger would pick one weapon to use. The defender didn't have permission to pick for himself. The challenger chose the weapon for him.

Martial arts of the time were practiced with a seriousness beyond an understanding we have today. One had to be physically and mentally ready for any type of violent encounter. It was necessary for one to keep in top physical shape and to keep one's skills polished. Rumor has it that Liu Seong was healthy enough over the decades to father one hundred children. However, the rumor doesn't concur with the noble standards of a Shaolin priest.

After Uncle Liu Seong's vision deteriorated, Willem became his representative. Liu Seong went into hiding for some months, intensely training his nephew. When Willem reached a high level of mastery, Liu Seong came out of hiding. Any challenges would be taken by his nephew from then on.

Willem with his uncle Liu Seong.
Photo courtesy of R. Lopez.

The early training at home and at the Shaolin Temple, prepared Willem for any potential encounters as he got older. An occasion often mentioned by American students was a large gathering of fighters in eastern Java. Willem had successfully defeated all adversaries. As a symbol of recognition, he was given a set of gold *taichu* (Jp. *sai*). Decades later, these were graphically included on his school patches and rank certificates.

Reeders' Military Service

Near the beginning of the Second World War, Japan invaded Indonesia. Reeders joined the Dutch Navy and was assigned to a naval ship to defend the coast of Java. When not fighting the Japanese, men on the ship organized boxing events during their free time. Reeders always came out on top, except once. He was knocked out after being struck in the head by an elbow. Reeders requested a rematch. In the first round, Reeders delivered a side kick to the boxer's throat. The opponent hit the floor and was unable to continue. The judge disqualified Reeders for using a technique forbidden by the boxing rules. The kuntao master exited off the floor with a grin.

There was not too much free time on the ship as the Japanese were always aggressive. A grave end came to Willem's ship when it was torpedoed and sunk in the shark infested harbor. Those of the Dutch crew who could abandon ship did and were soon picked up by a Japanese vessel. Supposedly Reeders resisted but was overtaken by twelve soldiers. All from the Dutch ship were taken prisoner.

Along with other prisoners, Reeders was transferred to a work camp. Here, somewhere along the 173-mile-long River Kwai in western Thailand, they were forced to build a bridge. Was this the same location as shown in the movie, The Bridge Over the River Kwai as some believe?

A slew of stories is associated with Reeders' interactions with the Japanese at this time. The first tale is of his escape, killing a few of the guards and jumping over the encampment fence to freedom. One of the guards was killed with a thunderous blow to his head with a knife-hand strike. Reeders recounts how he later removed some splintered skull bone fragments from his hand. Once out of the camp, he shaved his head and sometimes dressed as a Buddhist priest to blend in with the locals and not draw attention to himself.

Reeders joined up with other resistance fighters. One goal was to destroy the bridge he just helped build. He also went on to help other prisoners escape from other camps. Some of these stories were recorded by a journalist for *Action for Men* magazine and published in an article titled "Rampage of The Red Ant: Fantastic Saboteur Who Held Off a Jap Division."

Why the nickname? Red ants are noted to be highly aggressive, with an instinct to protect their territory. They will bite even when stepped on, injecting a venom into their attackers. They react quickly, attacking without pause until their opponent runs off or has died.

When Reeders was a prisoner of war in Nakhom Pathom, a city in central Thailand, he met Ernest de Vries, who was also a prisoner. De Vries was from Bogor in West Java, where an important Dutch administrative residency was located. It was also the summer capital of the Dutch East Indies. As a student of the famed pukulan master Mas Djut, bodyguard to the Sultan of Pontianak on Borneo. Reeders found a kindred spirit in de Vries. It was at this time that the contact with de Vries led to Reeders being introduced to many silat masters. De Vries' four nephews—Willem, Paul, Maurice and Victor de Thouars—and their father John, also became friends. The de Thouars brothers eventually moved to the U.S.

After the tide turned for the Japanese and they departed the area, the Indonesian populace ignited into a revolt against the Dutch. During their war for independence, Reeders found himself on the side of the Dutch. Officials heard of Reeders fighting behind enemy lines against the Japanese and recruited him for covert operations against the Indonesians. The officials wanted to negotiate with the leaders of the Independence movement. One rebel leader was named Koesno Sosrodihardjo, whom Reeders was to bring in for negotiations. Machine gun in hand, Reeders stealthily got close to this man, known as Sukarno. He felt Sukarno had a high spiritual presence. He withdrew without trying to bring Sukarno in for negotiation. The man he let go later became the first president of Indonesia, serving from 1945 to 1967.

A stamp printed in Indonesia shows President Sukarno, circa 1951.
ID 197648869
© Lefteris Papaulakis
Dreamstime.com

Leaving Indonesia

At the end of World War II, things were not well for the Dutch in the Netherlands. Weakened with little prospects of holding on to their colony, Indonesia obtained their freedom in 1949. The Wieling Plantation was confiscated by the Indonesian government and Reeders decided to move to the Netherlands. He spent a short time there, perhaps leaving after royal relatives pushed him into a marriage he didn't find comfortable. He left his wealth, wife, and perhaps children to live on another relative's plantation in South Africa—the cape colony once under Dutch rule (1652–1795 and 1803–1806), which afterwards came under the British. The situation here was not much better than in Indonesia.

Reeders did love hunting big game. Students in the U.S. said he used a 22-caliber rifle, a rifle more suitable for shooting squirrels than the large African animals. He no doubt used much more powerful rifles. He worked for a while as a hunting guide usually for rich British aristocrats. After one of his snooty clients died from a lion mauling, Reeders lost his job. Reeders didn't find reason to stay and departed for the Netherlands for a short time before landing in North America in the late 1950s.

A local church sponsored Reeders, helping him settle in Falconer, New York, a village situated just east of Jamestown. Unlike the story that he left his wife in the Netherlands; he was accompanied with his wife and children to New York state. He labored for a time in a furniture manufacturing plant to support his family. After getting to know the area better, he started teaching martial arts to locals. Class enrollment gradually grew.

First generation students from the Erie area regularly attended Reeders' classes in New York. This led to a conflict with Gerald Durant who had a large school in Erie where he taught Goju-Ryu karate that he had learned in Japan. He was losing students to Reeders and started gossiping about him. There was a confrontation in a dojo with Durant attacking repeatedly and ending up on the floor each time. Durant's students then attacked Reeders only to be dispersed. In the end, Reeders got more students and Durant became his friend.

Being close to Canada, Reeders had visited Toronto to enjoy the international atmosphere, especially in Chinatown. He made notable contacts, the most important being with Sam Wong (1936–

Reeders crouching on the far-left bottom in this photograph.
Jerry Bradigan on his right.

2014). Wong was born in Guangzhou, China, and studied with a Daoist monk named Ching Wan. The martial art he learned was associated with Wudong Mountain (武當山), a noted area of Daoist practices. He established the Mudong Kung Fu Club in Toronto in 1959, *mudong* being the Cantonese pronunciation of wudong.

Wong heard of Reeders' reputation and upon their first meeting, he thought the man before him didn't look even part Chinese and so challenged him to a fight as a test. Wong attacked and was immediately locked into an immovable position. Yes, the man before him was not an imposture, but the real Willem Reeders. Their friendship blossomed ever since. Eventually they created the Chong Hwa Kung Fu Hui (中華功夫會 Chinese Gongfu Association), an international federation of gongfu practitioners. Reeders was given the position of President and Chief Instructor (7th dan red sash) with the title of grandmaster. Sam Wong was an advisor, with Tan Kim Sjong serving as Vice President (based in Hong Kong), and Paul Tean as Chairman in Toronto.

A few times Richard Lopez drove Reeders to Toronto for visits. Reeders was welcomed in Wong's school as usual with open arms

Mudong Kung Fu Club gathering. Photos courtesy of www.nlsfmokwoon.com, Toronto, Canada.

as a martial art deity. Lopez as a non-Chinese was not allowed in. Sam Wong had a younger brother named Quai Wong. Because Quai was not born in China, he too was not allowed into his brother's school. Quai studied karate under Shoshin Nagamine.

A major disagreement developed between Reeders and others in the association around the traditional rule that non-Chinese should not be taught "real" gongfu. Reeders was open with his teachings and perhaps he shied away from the Toronto group because of the closed attitude he found among the masters there. He chose to teach in his own way in western New York.

On April 28, 1970, there was a large celebration for Reeders as reported in the *Evening Observer*, a Dunkirk-Fredonia newspaper. At the gathering came thirty Canadians from the Hong Luck School headed by Master Paul Chan and the Mudong Kung Fu Club headed by Sam Wong. Robert Servidio and others from the Erie area also attended. Public attendees were highly entertained to see many open-hand and weapons demonstrations. Those from Toronto were surprised to see how much Reeders' non-Chinese students were learning.

One day in Jamestown in the mid-1960s, two Chinese men arrived at Reeders' school. Reeders told all his students to go outside and wait. The men apparently were sent from Toronto to force Reeders to stop teaching non-Chinese. Somehow Reeders convinced them to leave unharmed. Students saw them sheepishly exit the building wearing terrified facial expressions. Reeders continued to teach as he wished but did include classes in karate and judo. It is said he eventually stopped publicly teaching his family kuntao in early 1966, passing on the art privately to a few students.

Royal Kung Fu seemed an appropriate name for Reeders to give his school: *kung fu* or *kuntao* simply refers to a martial art, and the royal term signifies his family and martial lineage. A 1971 newspaper clip shows a photograph and text recording a time when Reeders' sister came to visit him in the United States. She presented him with the House of Wieling royal title as a count and their coat of arms.

Many who knew Reeders personally can vouch for his supreme martial skills, including topnotch competitors in the national "karate circuit" the in 1960s. Few instructors from Southeast Asia were known to be teaching in America, but there was one known internationally because of his appearance in films. He was Danny Inosanto (b. 1936). It is reasonable that Inosanto would be attracted to Reeders' history and martial style. They are said to have met. Later Inosanto was to be the intermediary for introducing Bruce Lee to Reeders. According to oral history, Reeders gave Lee some instruction. Reeders shared stories that may have led to the original basis for the television program, Kung Fu, staring David Carradine (1936–2009). The plot was based on a young half-Chinese novice in the Shaolin Temple being taught by a blind monk.

Some say they did see proof that Reeders was in contact with Bruce Lee, through an exchange of letters written in Chinese. In Chinese, Americans may not have known who wrote the letters, or perhaps that they were viewing Chinese restaurant menus? —Sometimes what goes for proof is not what it seems.

Other stories emerged and you can compare accounts. Was it that Reeders studied at the Shaolin Temple in Hunan Province, Mount Tianmen in Hunan Province, or the Temple of Heaven in Beijing? Was he on staff as a Major with INTERPOL, the International

Criminal Police Organization? Did a mysterious monk teach Reeders usually by attacking him like Cato attacked Inspector Clouseau in the Pink Panter movies? Did he move to New Mexico because of a sinus condition or a malaria condition?

By the early 1970s Reeders had moved to Albuquerque, New Mexico, perhaps to find a climate more suitable for a chronic sinus condition. Most of his teachings now centered around pukulan and Tibetan Tai Chi. Perhaps he was going into semi-retirement and focusing more on health-related arts rather than the martial. He did have numerous problems from new and former students seeking the "real fighting art of kuntao." No doubt he wanted to keep a distance from the more fanatical practitioners.

Communications from students and family give Reeders' death year as 1989 or 1990. Perhaps the August 14, 1990 date is accurate. They say he went to Mexico for an operation for throat cancer. He was fond of smoking cigarettes, Dutch brands if available. The taste for cigarettes probably started while living on an Indonesian plantation where tobacco was a main crop. Reeders was cremated and his ashes dispersed in the Gulf of Mexico. Perhaps ocean currents brought ashes back to his place of birth.

Reeders' Martial Art Repertoire

The main art Reeders learned came from his uncle Liu Seong. As a Shaolin priest, the uncle must have been familiar with many styles practiced at the monastery. This includes a practice Reeders referred to as Tibetan Tai Chi. Reeders was one of a handful of young students chosen to study this unique art noted for nurturing health. He was the only one to complete the training, which included the final instructions given to him in Tibet. In the 1960s and 1970s, the term "tai chi" was sometimes used by Americans to mean "an exercise." The origin of what Reeders taught may have been derived from a martial-health practice in India.

He also inherited a family martial tradition via his uncle. There are a few photographs showing Reeders and his uncle practicing together. Later in the U.S., Reeders called his school Royal Kung Fu. Typical in Southeast Asia, he referred to his practice as kuntao, the term used in the region meaning "martial art". In Chinese mandarin it would be *kung fu*, which is now commonly Romanized as *gongfu*.

Reeders had the opportunity to meet and study with several silat masters. He established a good friendship with Ernest "Nes" de Vries, studying silat with him, Suro Djawan, Tji Petur, Lion de Riearere, Abu Saman, Theo Schrijn, Leo Sjel, Puk and Mancho Soverbier. Thus, Reeders assimilated silat styles including cikalong, cimande, harimau, and serak.

A famous Indonesian silat master of the time was Mas Djut (or Jud or Djoet), the founder of the Serak system. According to Victor de Thours, Reeders never studied with him directly, but did with Djut's students, Mas Roen and Teo Shrijin. Of all the silat masters mentioned, there is no record of the depth of study or length of time Reeders spent with them.

One account mentions that Reeders went to Mas Djut's gathering where silat practitioners were to fight. Reeders' name was put on the list to also fight. During his fight, Reeders threw a sidekick that sent his opponent flying ten yards where he landed lifeless.

Some accounts place Reeders studying at the Budokan in Tokyo, ranked 5th or 6th degree in Shotokan Karate, 7th degree in Budozen Soundje Kempo, and 10th degree in Kodokan Judo and Jujutsu, with some experience with aikido and kendo.

Reeders own system embodied what he most thoroughly absorbed, methods derived from the Chinese arts, silat and judo. His extraordinary experience entailed an assortment of weaponry of

ID 224388774 ©
Tigapagi Studio | Dreamstime.com

which he is said to have mastered eighty-one. He is often quoted as saying "Chinese hands and Indonesian feet" in reference to how he blended his own unique martial system upon kuntao and silat styles.

As mentioned earlier, "kuntao" simply refers to Chinese styles practiced in Southeast Asia. There are many styles of kuntao. The word "silat" refers to martial art styles as practiced in Southeast Asia. Likewise, there are many silat styles.

Reeders taught countless individual techniques, usually practiced in pairs. He also taught solo routines and defense against multiple attackers. His style makes great use of open-hand techniques, such as one-finger striking and spear-hand techniques. Every part of the body is considered a weapon and can be seen in the usage of attacks to vital areas and targets that leave an opponent crippled.

According to the first-generation students, Reeders did not have a set method of instruction. Plus, he taught different material to students at different times and in the various locations where he lived. Students couldn't be sure of the origins of particular techniques or routines. All were just part of the Reeders' system.

ID 48481072 © Narathip Ruksa | Dreamstime.com
ID 220331443 © Pramote Polyamate | Dreamstime.com

chapter III

An Alternate Reality

The content of the previous chapter was derived from what can be summed up as oral histories, hearsay, student writings, newspaper articles, websites and blogs, popular magazines, gossip and tales. In such cases, it isn't easy to know what is accurate. Sources may be unreliable, misinterpreted, misleading or only partially correct.

In this chapter, we will investigate documents and writings that present solid information about the life and teaching of Willem Reeders. These include documentation of life activities such as birth, marriage, divorce, immigration, occupation, military service, death, travel, and census.

The total amount of information obtained can be cross-referenced for accuracy. For example, a document may give a birthday as June 1, but eight other documents may give the day as July 1. When comparing the documents, we can guess that someone made a mistake and July 1st should be correct. Or we can just note that the two dates are possibilities, even though one is more probable.

As discussed earlier, during the 1950s and 1960s, a major problem for Americans interested in martial arts from a particular Asian country was that they were largely unfamiliar with its language, history and culture. In such cases, mistakes and misinterpretations are guaranteed. Compared with simple conversations, research needs to be more thorough, accurate and sound. Here in this chapter, we will use academic resources as books and articles, and other documents in English as well as records from the Netherlands, Indonesia, and Japan.

We have three main objectives for which we are seeking to find solid factual data to validate conclusions:

1) familial connections to Dutch and Chinese royalty
2) familial connections between Willem Reeders and Chinese relatives to establish the sources of the family martial system.
3) any other influences in martial studies from outside the family.

Paternal Lineage

According to genealogical records in the USA and the Netherlands, we find that Willem Andreas Reeders was born on 29 October 1917, in Surabaya, Indonesia. Surabaya is the capital city of East Java province and the second-largest city in Indonesia. Jakarta the capital and largest city is on the west side of the island, nearly five-hundred miles from Surabaya. At the time of Reeders' birth, the population of Surabaya was less than 200,000. Today it is close to three million.

The father of Willem was Cornelis Marinis Reeders. He was born on 27 August 1881, in a small village called Poortvliet in the Dutch province of Zeeland close to the North Sea. In 2021 its population was 1,715 and closer to 1,000 when Cornelis was born.

Although we expect to find a royal lineage, we learn from Dutch genealogical records that Cornelis' occupation was listed as a common laborer (www.genealogieonline.nl). Going back further, we find that his father, Willem's grandfather, was named Andreas Reeders, born 17 November 1847, in the village of Sint Maartensdijk, close to Poortvliet. It has a population today of 3,440. His occupation? — carpenter's apprentice (*timmermansknecht*) (www.genealogieonline.nl).

Andreas' wife was Adriana Wilhelmijna Slager, who was born on 8 July 1845, in Poortvliet. They were married on 9 February 1870, in Poortvliet. Sadly, she died on 4 March 1889, when just 44 years old. Andreas remarried to a woman named Johanna Philippina Suurland who was born on 26 April 1858.

Andreas' father, Cornelis Reeders, was born on 17 July 1818, in Sint-Maartensdijk. His occupation in 1842 was listed as a laborer, and in 1870 as a basketmaker (*mandenmaker*) (www.genealogieonline.nl). Cornelis had married Pieternella Hage, who was born on 6 January 1823. Her occupation was maid, a domestic helper (*huishoudelijke hulp*).

Cornelis' father, Willem's great great grandfather, was Andreas Reeders, born on 20 April 1773, in the small village of Zierikzee. It is on an island north of Sint Maartensdijk. It has about 10,000 population today. Like his son, Andreas is also listed as a basket-maker in 1842 (www.genealogieonline.nl).

From Willem Reeders paternal line, we find that his father moved from the Netherlands to Indonesia and married there. Before that were relatives living in the lowlands in the Netherlands. What has bearing on our understanding is that there is no mention of royal lineage through five generations, but of only laborers from small villages.

Maternal Lineage

Christina Helena Wieling, Willem's mother, was born on 9 January 1885, in Probolinggo, a port city 75 miles east of Surabaya. She married Cornelis on 22 February 1913, in Probolinggo. They had two other children besides Willem. The eldest was Adriana Engelina Reeders who was born on 10 April 1914. Willem's younger brother, Theo Cornelis Reeders, was born on 22 July 1920. Both siblings were also born in Surabaya.

Since Christina Wieling married into a family of laborers, it is most probable that she was not of royal lineage. Her father, Wybe Wieling, was born on 30 August 1873, in Berlikum, Netherlands.

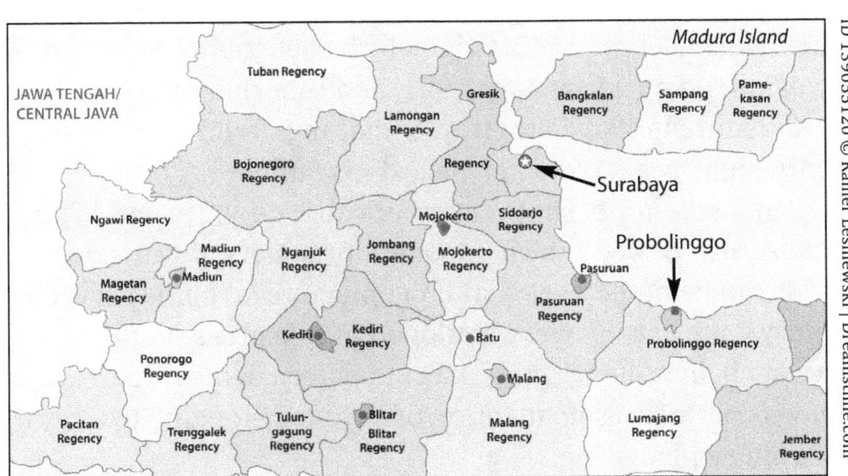

Berlikum is another small village with a population today of 2,529. Her mother, Margjen de Jong, was born on 24 September 1874, in Haskerdijken, at town about 24 miles south of Berlikum. Its population today is 375.

Christina's line can be traced back to her father and grandfather in the Netherlands. Her mother's side in the Netherlands also show no records of royalty. It seems she divorced and later married a man named Jippe de Vries on 28 May 1926. Willem's sister Adriana eventually moved to Groningen, Netherlands.

The most important facts concerning Christina is that both of her sons with her ex-husband were in Japanese prisoner of war (POW) camps. Japanese documents are included on the following pages with the first for Willem Reeders. It shows that he was serving in the Dutch navy for Observation Services, Armed Forces Second Army (渾軍二筴兵). He was captured on 12 March, year 17 of the Showa era (1942). Included here are his birth date, parents' names, and that he was captured in Java. By 8 August, he was in the Thai Prisoner of War Camp Number 6 (泰俘虜奴容所第 VI).

Willem's brother, Theo, was a Private First Class, assigned to the Main Dressing Station Department Surabaya Detachment. He too was captured in Java on 15 August 1942 but moved to a prisoner of war camp in Malaysia. His parents' names are listed. It is also noted that the United Nations forces have completed his extradition on 2 November 1946.

For Willem's father, the internment ended sadly. He held the rank of Retired Sergeant Major in the Royal Netherlands National Army. Evidently, he was captured and died in the Japanese camp in Ambarawa on 3 June 1945. Originally buried in Ambarawa, his body was exhumed on 11 January 1951, and reburied on 8 May 1951, in the Kalibanteng War Cemetery, Semarang, Indonesia. Willem was twenty-eight-years old when he lost his father.

On a side note, silat masters Ernest de Vries and Willem de Thouars also served time in Japanese prisoners of war camps.

It can be noted here that if people of royal blood served in the military, they usually were stationed in safe areas or didn't need to serve at all. In Willem's maternal and paternal lines, there are many siblings, but there is no mention of anyone belonging to a royal line or owning a plantation.

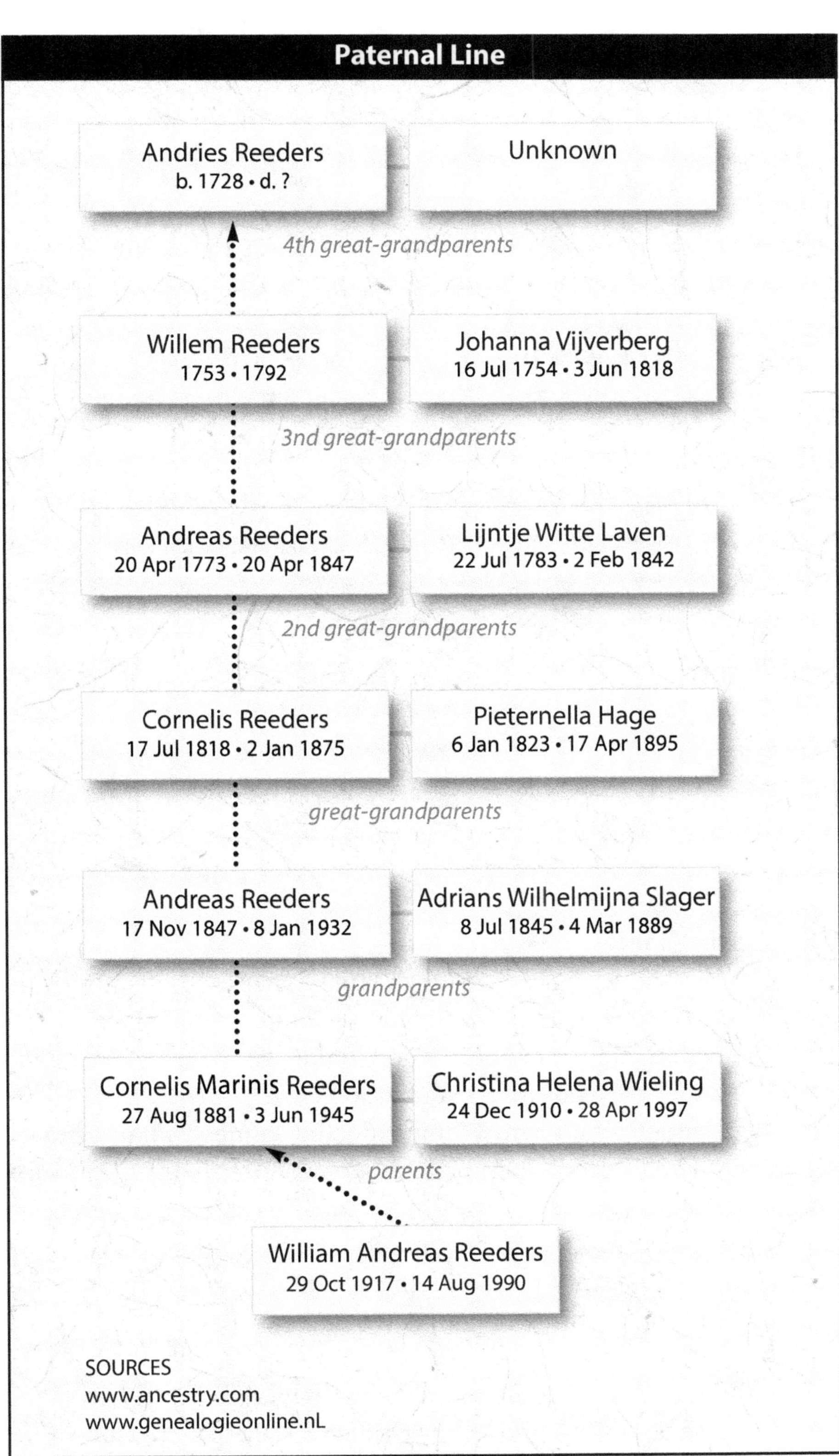

Andries Reeders
b. 1728 • d. ?

Unknown

4th great-grandparents

Willem Reeders
1753 • 1792

Johanna Vijverberg
16 Jul 1754 • 3 Jun 1818

3nd great-grandparents

Andreas Reeders
20 Apr 1773 • 20 Apr 1847

Lijntje Witte Laven
22 Jul 1783 • 2 Feb 1842

2nd great-grandparents

Cornelis Reeders
17 Jul 1818 • 2 Jan 1875

Pieternella Hage
6 Jan 1823 • 17 Apr 1895

great-grandparents

Andreas Reeders
17 Nov 1847 • 8 Jan 1932

Adrians Wilhelmijna Slager
8 Jul 1845 • 4 Mar 1889

grandparents

Cornelis Marinis Reeders
27 Aug 1881 • 3 Jun 1945

Christina Helena Wieling
24 Dec 1910 • 28 Apr 1997

parents

William Andreas Reeders
29 Oct 1917 • 14 Aug 1990

SOURCES
www.ancestry.com
www.genealogieonline.nL

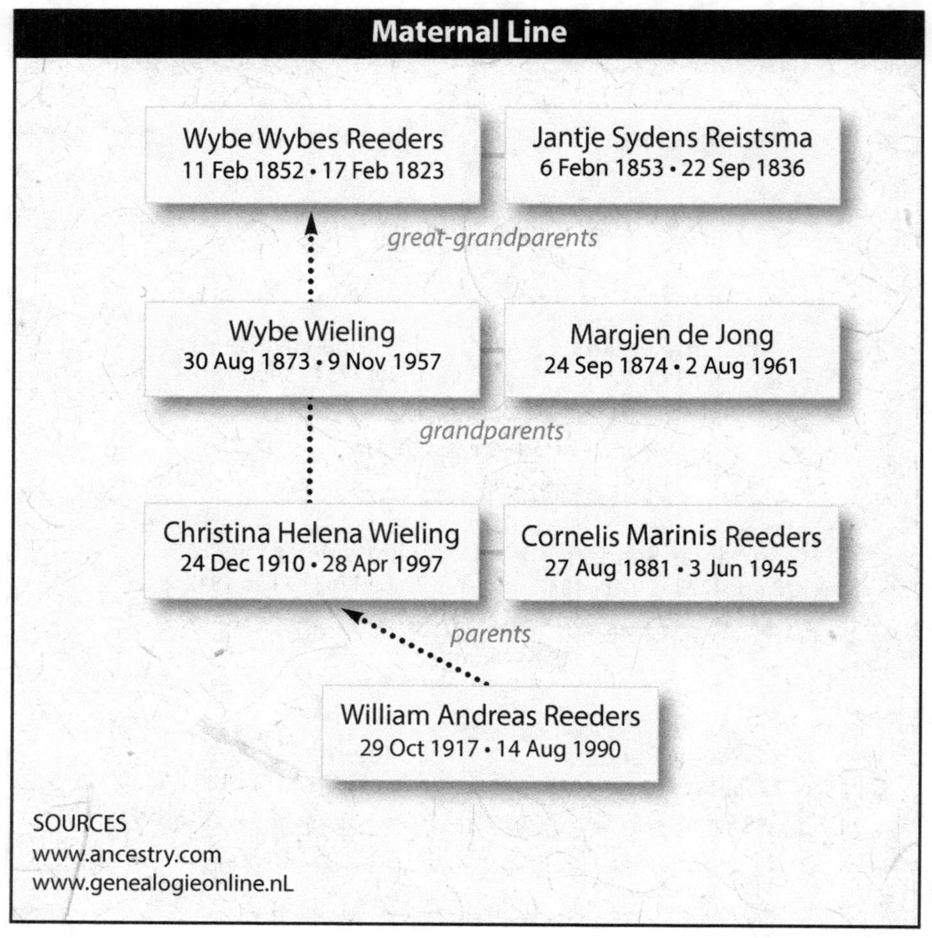

The Missing Link

When conducting research, what we don't find is as important as what we do find. When trying to find a Chinese blood relation for Willem Reeders, there is none. No documents support this long-held belief. But there are possible explanations.

Remember when Sam Wong expected to meet a half-Chinese half-Dutch Reeders in Toronto? He thought Willem was an imposter. Of course, Willem didn't have Chinese features: his parents were both Dutch according to all documents and bodily features. Even if there was a possibility that Willem's mother or grandmother was impregnated by a Chinese man, it would have been scandalously well-known.

In Chinese tradition, when a close friendship is established between two people, they may start giving family titles to each other.

For example, if two males become good friends, one of them would be called "uncle" by the other's children. Perhaps Liu Seong worked on the same plantation as Willem, even serving as the guard. During their free time, Reeders could have studied kuntao with him. It would have been normal for Willem to call him uncle, even if not blood related.

The name Liu Seong itself brings up questions. Chinese names usually consist of three characters: first is the surname, and the next two characters are the given name. Maybe Hap Kiem and Liu Seong are given names. What is their surname? In one case Liu Seong's was referred to in English as Liu Leo Seong, but it is unclear why or how three characters were derived.

On the Chinese Gongfu Federation (*Chong Hwa Kung Fu Hui*) certifications given by Reeders to students who became ranked as an orange sash or black belt, he signed his own name in Dutch above his printed name and "Liu Seong" in Chinese characters off to the lower left side.

There has been confusion on the spelling of "Liu Seong." Reeders and his students probably didn't know that there are a few different ways to Romanize Chinese. People often spelled as they thought a name was pronounced, even when the words were being pronounced differently. The characters Reeders used on the certificates are: 廖崇. In the modern Pinyin system, these are pronounced and Romanized as Liao (廖) Chong (崇). Liao is a common Chinese surname, but there is only one character for a given name.

Perhaps the *Liao Chong* combination is not a real name, but used as a nickname? *Liao* is a common surname by itself. *Chong* carries multiple meanings, including high, lofty, noble, esteemed, or to worship or adore. Together, *liao chong* may simply mean "Noble Liao."

Some westerners believe that Liu Seong was related to others with the same surname. Liu Yunqiao was a famous bajiquan master and instructor for Taiwan's Presidential bodyguards and special forces. He also had a great reputation as a covert operative in China. Just because his surname is Liu and he had an exceptional martial background doesn't mean he was related to Reeders. There are other examples that stem from this misunderstanding of Chinese names.

Southern Chinese dialects, as the Hakka dialect used by Reeders, pronounce characters differently than standard Mandarin. So the character 廖 may be pronounced as Liu both in Hakka and Liao in Mandarin. But the characters for the different surnames Liao (廖) and Liu (劉) are very different.

Are all people with the Liu surname related? It is the fourth common surname in mainland China, shared by approximately seventy million people. Is it possible that Willem's teacher's full name was Liu Liaochong (劉廖崇), whom he honored as an adopted uncle with the nickname of "Noble Liu"?

War's End and New Beginnings

A major change came for Willem when he married Marcella de Fretes (1923–2009) on February 26, 1946. She was born on June 3 in Cepu (formerly Tjepoe or Tjepu) on the northern part of Central Java. Her parents, Antonie de Fretes (1893–1930) and Jeanne Bakx (1897–1978), were both born in Semarang, Indonesia. Antonie's surname is of Portuguese origin. In 1511, Portugal became the first European country to explore Indonesia.

Passport documents for the newlyweds provide insightful information. The standard information includes full name, date of birth, place of birth, gender, details on parents, and a photograph. Their nationalities are listed as Nederlandse, and include the document numbers, and their signatures. The details were necessary to verify which Indo-Europeans were legally permitted to move from the now independent Indonesia to the Netherlands.

The passport papers for Marcella show her residence as:
Cultural Enterprise
% Pagergunung, Glenmore (Banyuwangi)

For Willem, it states that he was an:
Employee at David Birnie's
Administration Office
% Pagergunung, Glenmore (Banyuwangi)

Both were residing in Pagergunung, a village area located in the Glenmore district of Banyuwangi Regency, East Java. Today it is famous for it beautiful, rural landscape. During Reeders' time, it was in a region associated with bustling plantations.

What is this Administrative Office? It was the business headquarters for Dutchman Gerard David Birnie (aka Berny, 1862–1931) who was involved with the nationalization of plantations. Pagergunung is a sub-village within the village of Karangharjo in the Glenmore district of Banyuwangi, in East Java. This area is close to Mount Raung which produced fertile volcanic soils so suitable for plantations for producing cocoa, rubber, tea and coffee. Birnie secured rental rights from the colonial government in 1894 to develop the Ijen Highland.

Reeders is listed as being an employee at Birnie's plantation. It is not the Wieling Plantation we've heard about through hearsay. After World War II, the area gradually evolved from colonial possessions into modern Indonesian lands known for agriculture and tourism. In 1946, the Reeders had their passports in hand, ready to depart. The sovereignty of modern Indonesia was officially recognized on December 27, 1949.

The Dutch government was processing those whose documents showed that their nationalities were listed as Nederlandse. Marcella and Willem had the proper documentation. There are no known documents stating that they went to South Africa. It is logical that they did go directly to the Netherlands for a short time. It was the most convenient route to take post-World War II. Then during the early 1950s, they stayed for short periods in Falkner, Jamestown, and Dunkirk.

Some say that Marcella was a surgeon back in Indonesia and Willem was of royalty. In western New York, they lived in near poverty. Life was not easy and Marcella filed for divorce. In the early 1970s, Willem moved to Albuquerque, New Mexico. There he met Elann Michele Cronk (b. 1947) but separated in 1984. Soon after, Willem and his student, Marilyn Alexander (b. 1953) became domestic partners. They stayed together until his passing. Reeders' children made their homes in the Netherlands and the U.S.A.

泰　　　泰Ⅵ 㝹Ｉ 29395

収 容 所 Camp	泰　　昭17年 8 月 15日	番　　號 No.	Ⅲ 8108 4888
姓　名 Name	Reeders Wm. WILLEM ANDREAS. レーデルス ウイルム アンドレアス	生 年 月 日 Date of Birth	1917-10-29
國　籍 Nationality	蘭		
階級身分 Rank	Sailor Navy 海軍二等矢	所 屬 部 隊 Unit	10217 D Naval Observation Service
捕 獲 場 所 Place of Capture	爪哇	捕 獲 年 月 日 Date of Capture	昭和17 年 3 月 12日
父 ノ 名 Father's Name	Cornelis Marinus	母 ノ 名 Mother's Name	Christina
本 籍 地 Place of Origin	Soerabaia D.E.I.	職　　業 Occupation	鉄道局従業員
通 報 先 Destination of Report	Tjempatrastraat nr.6 Soerabaia	特 記 事 項 Remark	

補 修 欄　Other Informations
昭和18 年 月 日 泰俘虜収容所第Ⅵ 分所ヘ移營ス
昭和20年 8月 30日バンコックニ於テ聯合國軍ニ引渡ス

収 容 所 Camp	昭和17 年 8 月 15日	番 號 No.	
姓 名 Name	Reeders, Theo リーデルス，テオ．	生 年 月 日 Date of Birth	1920-7-22
國 籍 Nationality		所 屬 部 隊 Unit	No. 124620 Hoofdverbandplaatsafdeling Detachement Soerabaja.
階 級 身 分 Rank	Soldaat 2e Klasse 陸軍二等兵		
捕 獲 場 所 Place of Capture	爪哇	捕 獲 年 月 日 Date of Capture	昭和 17 年 3 月 9 日
父 ノ 名 Father's Name	C.M. Reeders	母 ノ 名 Mother's Name	Chr. Wieling
本 籍 地 Place of Origin	Soerabaja	職 業 Occupation	
通 報 先 Destination of Report	C.M. Reeders Heerenstraat 16, Probolinggo.	特 記 事 項 Remarks	32582

補 修 欄 Other Informations
18.9.26,
昭和20年 11月 2日 聯合國軍二引渡完了ス

War records for
Cornelis Marinis Reeders
(27 Aug 1881 • 3 Jun 1945)

Rank: Retired Sergeant Major
in the Royal Netherlands
National Army.

Captured and died in the Japanese camp in Ambarawa on 3 June 1945. Originally buried in Ambarawa, his body was exhumed on 11 January 1951, and reburied on 8 May 1951, in the Ereveld Kalibanteng War Cemetery, Semarang, Indonesia.

Grafnummer: M. III 10	Begraafplaats: Ereveld K... Banteng	Letter: R

DUPLICAAT

		Gegevens afkomstig van:
Naam	: REEDERS	1) O.D.O.
Voornamen (letters)	: Cornelis Marinus	
Landaard (Nationaliteit)	: Nederlander	
Rang (functie)	: Gep. Sgt. Majoor Genie (Conducteur)	
Stamboek Nr.	: Kampno. 21289	
Geboortedatum (ouderdom)	: 27-8-1881	
Geboorteplaats	: Poortvliet	Wed:
Plaats en datum van overlijden	: Ambarawa dd. 3-6-1945	C. Reeders - Wieking
Geloof	: Rooms Katholiek Ned Hervormd	Oosterhamrikkade 95 A
Doodsoorzaak	:	Groningen
Naaste familie	: Wed. Chr. Reeders-Wieling Ook Ha...	
Bijzonderheden	: Oorspronkelijk begraven te Ambarawa.	
	Opgraving dd. 11-1-1951	
	Herbegraven dd. 8-5-1951	
	Acte B.S. 8016/1946 te Djakarta.	

Repr. Djatop. 9551B. 4.000 Ib./'55.

INHOUDSOPGAVE

Naam _Reeders_

Voornamen _Cornelis Marinus_

Geboren te _Poortvliet_ d.d. _27-8-1881_

Begraven te _Kalibanteng_ Land _Ind._

O O R L O G S G R A V E N S T I C H T I N G

Bankaplein 5 – 's-Gravenhage – Telefoon 541300

Ind./dG.   'S-GRAVENHAGE, *6-9-'62*

> U wordt verzocht deze vragenlijst
> nauwkeurig in te vullen.

1. Naam: *Reeders*
2. Voornamen: *Cornelis Marinus*
3. Datum en plaats van geboorte: *27-8-1881 Poortvliet*
4. Datum en plaats van overlijden: *3 Juni 1945 – Ambarawa kamp. 7.*
5. Plaats van begraven: *eregraf. – Semarang.*
6. Kerkgenootschap: *Ned. Hervormd*
7. Militaire rang óf burger functie: *gep. sergt. Majoor Coml. 2e kl. Gen.*
8. Legernr.: *5 4837*
9. Bijzonderheden: *geen.*

Wij verzoeken U dit formulier terug te zenden, <u>óók</u> indien U niets of weinig bekend is.

A a n : *Wed: C. Reeders - Wieling*
Oosterhamrikkade 95A
Groningen

(okletters): **REEDERS**

WILLEM, ANDREAS

Reg. No. 54

..: 29 October 1917   plaats: SURABAIA   land: INDONESIA

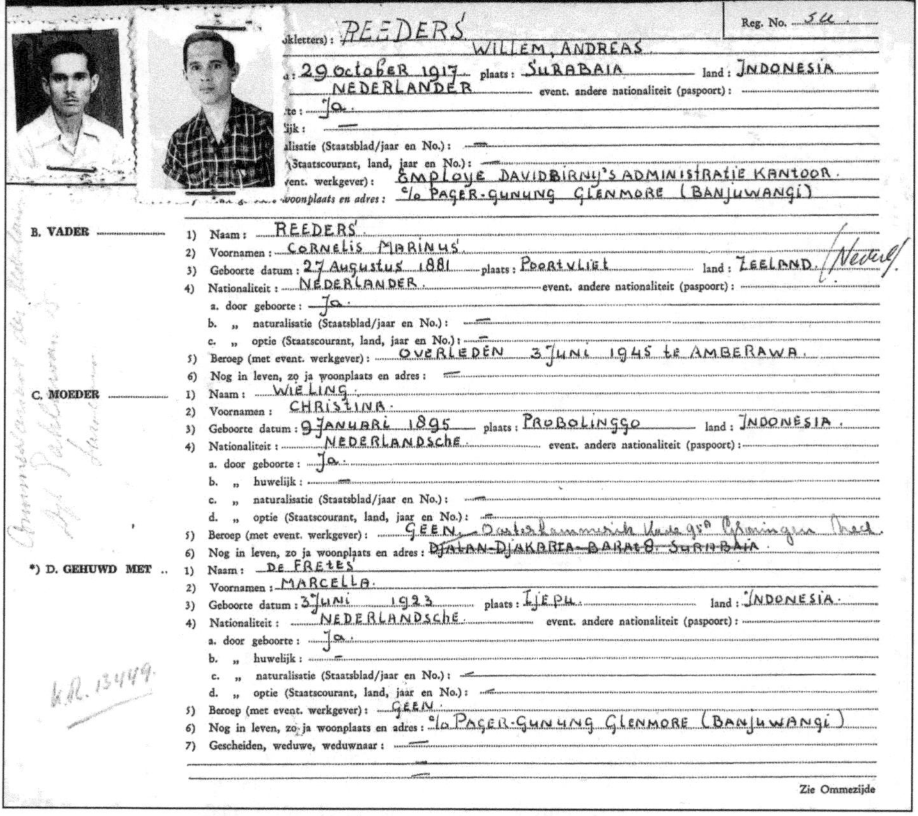

NEDERLANDER   event. andere nationaliteit (paspoort): ...

..te: Ja.

..lijk: ...

..alisatie (Staatsblad/jaar en No.): ...

(Staatscourant, land, jaar en No.): ...

(event. werkgever): EMPLOYE DAVIDBIRNY'S ADMINISTRATIE KANTOOR.

..woonplaats en adres: c/o PAGER-GUNUNG GLENMORE (BANJUWANGI)

B. VADER

1) Naam: REEDERS'
2) Voornamen: CORNELIS MARINUS'
3) Geboorte datum: 27 Augustus 1881   plaats: Poortvliet   land: ZEELAND. (Nederl.)
4) Nationaliteit: NEDERLANDER   event. andere nationaliteit (paspoort): ...
   a. door geboorte: Ja.
   b. „ naturalisatie (Staatsblad/jaar en No.): ...
   c. „ optie (Staatscourant, land, jaar en No.): ...
5) Beroep (met event. werkgever): OVERLEDEN 3 Juni 1945 te AMBERAWA.
6) Nog in leven, zo ja woonplaats en adres: ...

C. MOEDER

1) Naam: WIELING
2) Voornamen: CHRISTINA.
3) Geboorte datum: 9 Januari 1895   plaats: PROBOLINGGO   land: INDONESIA.
4) Nationaliteit: NEDERLANDSCHE   event. andere nationaliteit (paspoort): ...
   a. door geboorte: Ja.
   b. „ huwelijk: ...
   c. „ naturalisatie (Staatsblad/jaar en No.): ...
   d. „ optie (Staatscourant, land, jaar en No.): ...
5) Beroep (met event. werkgever): GEEN. Oostkammerik Krieg 9e Groningen (Ned.)
6) Nog in leven, zo ja woonplaats en adres: DJALAN-DJAKARTA-BARAT 8 SURABAIA

***) D. GEHUWD MET ..**

1) Naam: DE FRETES'
2) Voornamen: MARCELLA.
3) Geboorte datum: 3 Juni 1923   plaats: Ijepu   land: INDONESIA.
4) Nationaliteit: NEDERLANDSCHE   event. andere nationaliteit (paspoort): ...
   a. door geboorte: Ja.
   b. „ huwelijk: ...
   c. „ naturalisatie (Staatsblad/jaar en No.): ...
   d. „ optie (Staatscourant, land, jaar en No.): ...
5) Beroep (met event. werkgever): GEEN.
6) Nog in leven, zo ja woonplaats en adres: c/o PAGER-GUNUNG GLENMORE (BANJUWANGI)
7) Gescheiden, weduwe, weduwnaar: ...

K.R. 13449.

Zie Ommezijde

Reg. No. ....

..........) : REEDERS — DE FRETES.
MARCELLA.
3 JUNI-1923. plaats : TJEPU land : INDONESIE.
NEDERLANDSE. event. andere nationaliteit (paspoort) : ....
JA — M. Bangkok. 26-2-1946.
(Staatsblad/jaar en No.) : ....
......courant, land, jaar en No.) : ....
......werkgever) : ....
......ts en adres : CULTUUR-ONDERNEMING PAGGER-GUNUNG. GLENMORE.(BANJUWANGI).

B. VADER

1) Naam : DE FRETES.
2) Voornamen : ANTHONIUS.
3) Geboorte datum : 9 DECEMBER 1898 plaats : SURAKARTA land : INDONESIE.
4) Nationaliteit : event. andere nationaliteit (paspoort) :
   a. door geboorte : JA.
   b. „ naturalisatie (Staatsblad/jaar en No.) :
   c. „ optie (Staatscourant, land, jaar en No.) : OVERLEDEN. TE SEMARANG. 1930.
5) Beroep (met event. werkgever) :
6) Nog in leven, zo ja woonplaats en adres :

C. MOEDER

1) Naam : BAKX
2) Voornamen : JEANNE.
3) Geboorte datum : 12 AUGUSTUS 1900. plaats : SEMARANG. land : INDONESIE.
4) Nationaliteit : NEDERLANDSE. event. andere nationaliteit (paspoort) :
   a. door geboorte : JA
   b. „ huwelijk : J—
   c. „ naturalisatie (Staatsblad/jaar en No.) :
   d. „ optie (Staatscourant, land, jaar en No.) :
5) Beroep (met event. werkgever) : Gubeng Gang kembi 1 Surabaia
6) Nog in leven, zo ja woonplaats en adres : PERAK BOULEVARD 225 SURABAIA.

***) D. GEHUWD MET ..**

1) Naam : REEDERS.
2) Voornamen : WILLEM, ANDREAS.
3) Geboorte datum : 29 OCTOBER 1917 plaats : SURABAIA. land : INDONESIE.
4) Nationaliteit : NEDERLANDER. event. andere nationaliteit (paspoort) :
   a. door geboorte : JA
   b. „ huwelijk :
   c. „ naturalisatie (Staatsblad/jaar en No.) :
   d. „ optie (Staatscourant, land, jaar en No.) :
5) Beroep (met event. werkgever) : CO PAGGER EMPLOYE . D.B.A.K.
6) Nog in leven, zo ja woonplaats en adres : CO PAGGER - GUNUNG. GLENMORE. BANJUWANG
7) Gescheiden, weduwe, weduwnaar :

Gehuwd te Nelson Pathom 26-10-1946

(left margin notes:)
Geboorte N. 379/1917
B. J. Surabaia.
Vader :
Cornelis Marinus Reeders 1849
geb. 29 Aug. 1881.
Poortvliet

Zie Ommezijde

William Andreas Reeders
29 Oct 1917 • 14 Aug 1990

Marcella de Fretes
3 Jun 1923 • 26 Jan 2009

LIST OF ANNOTATIONS

NO.	NAME.	NAAM.	REF.
1.	Breakwater	Havendam	047 291
2.	Stores	Pakhuisen	046 285
3.	Stores	Pakhuisen	045 278
4.	Slipway	Sleephelling	046 282
5.	Coal Stacks	Kolenstapels	047 284
6.	Coal Stacks	Kolenstapels	045 282
7.	Coal Stacks	Kolenstapels	047 277
8.	Prison	Gevangenis	046 268
9.	Rice Bag Factory	Rijstzakken Fabriek	046 271
10.	Mosque	Moskee	044 269
11.	Railway Station	Spoorwegstation	045 271
12.	Hospital	Hospitaal	039 268
13.	Regent's Residence	Regentswoning	045 267
14.	Assistant Resident	Assistent Resident	044 258
15.	Training College	Kweekschool	043 266
16.	Mulo School	Mulo School	043 265
17.	Police Barracks	Politie Kaserne	043 267
18.	Post & Telegraph Office	Post en Telegraaf Kantoor	045 264
19.	Club	Societeit	045 261
20.	Roman Catholic Church	R.K. Kerk	045 260
21.	Hotel	Hotel	044 261
22.	Hotel	Hotel	046 259
23.	Market	Markt	047 259
24.	Market	Markt	048 257
25.	Molasses Store	Molasse pakhuizen	053 258
26.	Molasses Store	Molasse pakhuizen	054 259
27.	Molasses Store	Molasse pakhuizen	056 258
28.	Rice Mill	Rijst Pellerij	053 255
29.	Steamtram Co. Depot.	Stoomtram Mij. Depot.	054 256
30.	District Officer	Controleur	039 259
31.	Controleur	Controleur	040 258
32.	Christian Bros. School	Christelijke Broeders School	034 257
33.	Technical School	Technische School	044 254
34.	Churchyard	Kerkhof	050 257
35.	Ship Building Yards	Scheepswerven	037 271
36.	Rice Bag Factory	Rijstzakken Fabriek	059 258

Dutch Translations by ISTD(SEAC)

Distributed by the Government of Republic of Indonesia.

chapter 4

A Hybrid Conception of a Man and His Art

Chapter one in this book gives the historical and cultural backdrop for us to get an understanding of what society was like when Willem Reeders was living in Java. While chapter two presents many of the Reeders' lore that blossomed over his decades living in the United States, chapter three focuses on the facts obtained by reliable research and verifiable personal accounts. What happens if we utilize the historical and factual chapters to sieve through the stories of chapter two?

The most important facts obtained about Willem Reeders help us discern what is true and accurate verses what is the substance of legend. We start at the beginning with Willem's birth in the bustling Islamic port of Surabaya, Java, on 29 October 1917. It's the same city where his siblings were born. It was a Dutch economic and military base for centuries with anti-Dutch sentiments constantly in the atmosphere. Sukarno, the future president of Indonesia, went to school and worked there. It is where the main battle for Indonesian independence took place.

Probolinggo city may be more important for the Reeders family, since it was where Willem's mother Christina Helena Wieling was born to Dutch parents. This is the coastal city where she married Willem's father Cornelis in 1913. She later married Jippe de Vries in 1926, when Willem was only thirteen years old. Why did she get divorced? Did her husband Cornelis discover Willem was not his, and the result of an affair with a Chinese man?

Surabaya and Probolinggo were long known as ports associated with crime and corruption, not to mention their place in regional and major international conflicts. In Willem's time, he saw the Dutch wrestle to maintain their influence there, even as the Japanese took over the area. Also, during Willem's early years, he would easily become fascinated with the mythical stories and the multi-cultural elements that included aspects of the supernatural. The Chinese population had their businesses, temples, and martial exhibitions. The magical and martial shows displayed techniques promised to empower a warrior. Amulets and prayers were believed to protect one from sickness and violent attack.

Rather than a life of riches among the laboring class in Probolinggo, documents from the Netherlands and Indonesia show a different status for the Reeders family. Willem's father Cornelis is listed as a common laborer. Going back generations, we find that Willem's grandfather Andreas was a carpenter's apprentice; his great grandfather Cornelis was a basketmaker whose wife Pieternella was a domestic helper; and even his great great grandfather Andreas worked as a basketmaker. Basketmaking was valued in the Netherlands and perhaps more so in Java. For example, the varied designs were used in the fish and fruit markets, and on plantations to carry coffee beans, tobacco leaves and other products.

The ancestral line for Willem's mother, Christina Wieling, can be traced back to her father and grandfather in the Netherlands. Her mother's side was also in the Netherlands. All were from small villages, and no records of royalty lineage are found. Plus, since Cornelis was from a line of common laborers, she is predictably of the same class.

For Willem's recent ancestry of three generations, we find the surnames of Reeders, Wieling, de Jong, Slager, Reistsma, and Hage. None are connected to the Dutch royal family of Karl Lodewygk. Without a royal status, Willem would not have been privy to the Chinese connections as believed in the Reeders legends.

The relationship with "uncle" Liu Seong may be based on a close friendship with a Chinese martial artist in Java. If Willem started his martial studies at age four when his "uncle" was eighty or one hundred years old according to recounts, it seems impossible for a blind old man to make annual visits to the Shaolin

Monastery over a ten-year period. If he was eighty years old when he started to teach young Willem, he would have been ninety years old for the last trip into China.

Now we must ask what Willem was doing in Java before the war with the Japanese and the war of Indonesian independence. Was he living the life of royalty on the Wieling Plantation as believed by generations in the Reeders' kuntao lineage state? According to his passport records, he and his wife Marcella were employed on a plantation run by David Birnie. It is in Pagergunung, Glenmore (Banyuwangi), a sub-village within the village of Karangharjo. This is about 115 miles (186km) southeast from Probolinggo.

Birnie was a well-known Dutchman famous for starting and developing commercial agriculture in Java, beginning with a coffee plantation in Bondowoso. His work greatly changed the society around his far-reaching programs. He employed many to work the fields, maintain buildings and machinery, and attend to administrative duties.

Other stories do not follow a logical timeline. Considering the circumstances in Java while Willem was young enough to study for an engineering degree, when and where was this possible? University-level education did not exist in Indonesia until 1920 and started with only a few students. When he was of college age, the Japanese were exerting their influence in Indonesia. Willem was serving in the navy and captured in March of 1942. His father was interned and died in the Ambarawa camp when Willem was twenty-eight-years old. This was one of the camps from which the British evacuated European and Indo-European internees after Japan was defeated.

At the end of World War II in 1949, Willem was thirty-two years old. After all that happened on the island of Java and to his own family, Willem would never think to go study judo at the Budokan in Tokyo. After all, he, his father and brother suffered under the brutal hands of the Japanese military as their prisoners of war. With the help of the Dutch government, he was fortunately able to go to the Netherlands with his wife Marcella de Fretes, later emigrating to the United States.

When Reeders was relocated with the help of a church in Falconer, New York, he needed income for his growing family. He probably obtained some skills from his father and later by working on the plantation in Pagergunung. He could build things. Hence, without a command of the English language, he was an "engineer" in the sense of a craftsman as his ancestors were. In Jamestown, New York, he worked in a furniture factory. He quit that job, finding it more convenient to teach martial arts for a living.

If Liu Seong was Willem's main source of martial knowledge, we remain puzzled by their exact relationship. It's most probable that Liu Seong was employed as a guard on the Pagergunung plantation and he took Willem under his wing. As far as his studies of silat, he certainly met Ernest de Vries and other silat masters. He probably met other Chinese and Japanese martial artists too. Whenever an opportunity arose to meet a martial expert, Reeders was a quick study compared with mere mortals.

To learn a martial art system takes much time and effort, the very meaning of the words "kung fu/gongfu." It is illogical to think that Reeders studied all the styles accredited to him: Chinese kuntao and Tibetan Tai Chi: silat styles of cikalong, cimande, harimau, and serak; Japanese styles of karate, aikido, kempo, judo, jujutsu, and kendo; and mastery of eighty-one weapons. But there is a good reason for people to believe he did master all these.

Usually someone who studies a martial art focuses on one style for a lifetime. There may be some exposure to other styles. Fighting systems may be known for their specific technical focus, such as a grappling, striking, kicking, throwing, or using a particular weapon. Especially in recent years, many individuals dabble in numerous arts. The bottom line is that a person only has so much time to devote to martial studies and absorb what is humanly possible. As a result, we find only a few gifted people who have mastered more than one or two styles.

In Willem Reeders' case, it seems he came to master a universal art of combat. He intuitively grasped the underlying principles upon which all martial art styles are based. He understood the essentials of gravity, balance, speed, timing, and leverage. He utilized body mechanics and the array of natural human weapons, including fingers, hands, knees, elbows, and shoulders. The body was his weapon, guided by his mental powers. Movement was directed by highly developed sensitivity and awareness, especially in relationship to himself, opponents, and the environment.

For Reeders, the combat system he embodied was encompassing, a hybrid art beyond the scope of what even other gifted practitioners could grasp. His style was beyond simply a blend of Chinese and Indonesian styles. By mastering the principles of the universal art of combat, any style or weapon could be easily adapted into his repertoire.

The complexity of martial art styles can be understood by using a simple analogy. We know that presently there are over seven thousand living languages. How many languages do you speak? One? Perhaps two? Amazingly, there are people who learn to speak five, even ten languages. A rare few can speak up to fifty languages. There are commonalities in all these language as defined by basic grammar—starting with the person speaking, those spoken to, and objects spoken about. The essentials are key to grasping how all languages work. The same can be said of the martial arts.

The stories weaved around Willem Reeders' life reflect a

search for identity, much like the Indonesian search for national identity. Both the man and the country inherited extreme cultural diversity—from religions to political parties. Additionally, there were outbreaks of war, disease, famines, and other natural disasters. Both man and country fought to survive during the first half of the twentieth century. Myths from the past inspired and gave strength, supported by beliefs in spiritual powers.

The people of Indonesia found commonality underlying their diversity, surviving hundreds of years of exploitation to finally establish their own country. It seems Willem Reeders also went through his own personal struggles to survive. Today the topic of post-traumatic stress disorder (PTSD) explains the results of post-war syndrome of veterans, including flashbacks, severe anxiety and depression. This is only one aspect that may have affected his life. By itself, emigrating is a struggle for anyone to experience. What else did this man bear?

Many of the Reeders legends may have arisen to make sense out of a chaotic past. Story telling is a deep Indonesian tradition. This is the stuff of legends, based on historical events but unauthenticated, as shown in the legend of King Author, for example. We can sort out what we've read and heard about Reeders into what is (1) reliable fact, (2) fiction, or (3) what falls into the category of the undetermined.

In the end, many of the myths around Reeders are not of supreme importance, although attention grabbing. What we know for sure is that he was a martial art prodigy. The origins of the word prodigy prove insightful. It stems from the Latin *prodigium*, meaning a prophetic sign, omen, or portent. The word was used to single out something as extraordinary, being an unnatural occurrence. Reeders' martial teachings have touched and inspired many. His life story offers a rare view of one of the most gifted martial artists of the twentieth century.

chapter V

Reeders' Hybrid Fighting System

The Font of Martial Knowledge

Just where and from whom did Willem Reeders obtain his encyclopedic knowledge about martial arts has been covered in the previous chapters. We can concisely recount the information here relating to three sources: 1) Liu Seong, 2) silat practitioners in Java, and 3) other unidentified influences.

Liu Seong, Romanized according to standard Mandarin as Liao Cong (廖崇), remains a mysterious figure. The Chinese characters for his name were found on ranking certificates Reeders gave to his senior students (see page 88). According to all ancestral documentation, Liu Seong does not appear to be a blood relative. It is more likely that he was an intimate friend and mentor to Willem and, according to Chinese custom, would have established an "uncle-nephew" relationship.

Another theory is that Willem Reeders' mother, grandmother or grandfather had a child outside of wedlock. This wouldn't be totally unusual at that time, but there is absolutely no proof that it occurred. Willem's mother Christina is shown to have married twice, both times to Dutchmen. His grandmother, Margjen de Jong, had Dutch parents. His grandfather Wybe Wieling also had Dutch parents. Did he have a child with a Chinese woman? Again, there is no documentation to support such theories. The best way to know for sure would be for living children or grandchildren to take a DNA test from such companies as Ancestry.com and MyHeritage DNA.

Regardless of the actual identity of Liu Seong, he was certainly the most influential teacher for Reeders. He was the font of his kuntao knowledge. The other martial arts that Willem came to learn were filtered through his kuntao and adapted into a personal hybrid system unlike any other practitioner.

Ernest de Vries is another key figure in Willem's martial heritage. They were close enough to share material and practice together with Liu Seong. It's natural that de Vries would reciprocate and introduce Reeders to his pukulan master Mas Djut and others. So, even in relatively short periods, Willem had the unique ability to grasp various silat styles to add to his stock of martial techniques.

What allowed Reeders to absorb styles so quickly was that he has a savant—having an exceptional aptitude for learning combat-related skills. Living in Indonesia, he had the opportunity to meet other Chinese and Indonesian masters. Perhaps he also met some Japanese masters who were in Java during their early years developing business and trade relations or even during the war period.

In the end, by focusing on underlying principles of combat arts, Reeders embodied a universal art of combat. All martial movements—strikes, kicks, locks, throws, breaks, sweeps, blocks, deflections, etc.—work according to fundamental physical laws. Reeders didn't just master a system; he mastered the underlying essentials of fighting arts.

Personal Theory of Self-Defense

Most martial artists today are motivated to practice for various reasons. Many are involved for the competitive element, enjoying tournaments and sparring for trophies. Others, particularly the elderly, may wish to nurture their health by keeping flexible and toned through their movements. A small number of practitioners are interested in the practical applications for self-defense, especially useful for people working in law enforcement and in the military. Usually, the later are practicing in the most realistic ways to test their efficiency.

Reeders had reasons to learn what was most practical for real combat. Being Dutch, he dealt with social bias everywhere he went. There were regular skirmishes among locals as well as clashes between foreign and regional groups. The ultimate threat came from the brutal Japanese occupation during decades of Reeders' life in Java. A potential lethal encounter came each day. Reeders prepared for this.

The goal was simply to survive by finishing an opponent as quickly as possible, leaving absolutely no opportunity for the opponent to be a threat again. This killing mindset guided practice involving the whole human condition of body, mind, and spirit. This was martial arts beyond competition. There was no concern for a winning point or possessing a gold-plated trophy.

Reeders developed his body through training. Robert Servidio drove him to a doctor's office for a physical in Erie, Pennsylvania. When the doctor found that his patient was in such extraordinary condition, he yelled for Servidio to enter the examination room to explain how it was possible Reeders was in Olympic condition. Servidio responded: "He's a martial artist who practices regularly."

The special mental and spiritual traits are much more difficult to understand than the physical. Reeders could do things that others could not that relied on cultivating the inner self. Many talk about "internal styles" but have little to show for it. Reeders could move as if he had foreknowledge, a precognition of what would happen before it did. He would know how an opponent would attack beforehand. Therefore, he'd easily move out of the way to safety and simultaneously devastate his opponent.

In Indonesia, martial artists sometimes display talents beyond the norm. Dr. Michael Malizewski, a psychologist and former editor for the *Journal of Asian Martial Arts,* travelled to Indonesia to investigate the paranormal skills of practitioners. In personal discussions, individuals would show him various ways they would test their own abilities. These included: holding a burning torch under their forearms without getting burned; taking razor blades out of their paper wrapping, chewing them into pieces, swallowing, then regurgitating the pieces; cutting paper and banana leaves with razor blades and knives, then drawing the edges across their skin without being cut themselves.

Dr. Maliszewski talked about this and shared a film taken during his travels. For centuries there has been a fusion of martial arts with the mystic practices as found in ancient native rituals and those from Hinduism, Buddhism, and Islam. Belief in these spiritual traditions have an effect. Heck, even Nike says, "Just Do It!"

In addition to practicing martial techniques, there is an assortment of associated practices devoted to spiritual development. These include deep breathing techniques, fasting, selective dieting, inducing trance states, and practicing meditations. There is a wide variety of practices. There is no uniform system, so each religious and martial sect are different. Javanese mysticism in particular lacks a systematic theology.

The final stage of training in silat is referred to as *kebatinan,* referring to the occult conditions a practitioner attains. The common term for teacher is *guru,* but the title of *pendekar* ("skilled duelist") is reserved for those who have reached into the spiritual levels. The title "connotes spiritualist and leader or champion who has obtained an understanding of true [inner] knowledge. . . *pandai akal,* ability in the sense of complete feeling combined with mind (Maliszewski, 1992:27).

The higher levels of training offer many abilities. Maliszewski sums up:

> Capabilities reported by practitioners of these techniques include mystic healing, mind reading, precognition, the ability to disable an opponent by touch, identification with and emulation of the characteristics of certain animals, the ability to place spells on enemies, combat invulnerability, and even the power to "kill at a distance" (Maliszewski, 1992:27).

Of course, all such attributes are also claimed by charlatans, who greatly outnumber any of those possessing true skills. Regardless, the mental/spiritual aspects are significantly more important than sole physical skills. Even if these more intangible dimensions are dubious, they capture the imagination to possibilities beyond the norm.

The physical techniques Reeders taught and showed through many public and private demonstrations are profound. He talked about the mental/spiritual aspects as well, but to a selective group. We can only grasp hints of his knowledge in this area. It is good to keep in mind that he was influenced by the longstanding presence of the mystical traditions that form a vital element in Indonesian culture.

Essential Skills

Reeders was like Santa Clause who could select from his bag of goodies just what technique he thought appropriate to teach each individual or group. Many try to classify these techniques as coming from specific styles, but the lines separating them are not very clear. It is easier to look at his teaching as including a range of techniques from the basic to most advanced. The advanced are built upon the basics, so what may seem simplistic just may be the most profound.

As noted earlier, Reeders did not have a standardized syllabus. No standardization. No organized way of teaching, except for what he felt like teaching at a certain time and place. This probably was a way to test students' personalities and skills, and to guard his most cherished knowledge.

Basic techniques were taught to perform solo and with a partner. Repeating one technique many many times ensured improvement. Sometimes the work on one technique went on for weeks or months before moving on to another technique. Dedicated students noticed the effects. Their basics got better and their variety of techniques increased.

An essential for learning the techniques properly was to spar, not for points or trophies, but to improve speed, accuracy, and power. Take chances. Learn your limitations. Moving spontaneously to an unpredictable opponent while training distancing and awareness. Was an opponent's movement just a distraction? When to move in or out?

Each opponent is different in physical build and technical experience. Learn from each situation and look to yourself for improvement—like the archer who misses the target does not blame the bow or arrow. He looks at himself. Take the opportunity to learn from each minute of practice.

As opponents vary, so do the surroundings. Note the conditions, such as weather, terrain, and lighting. It is important to maintain one's balance and control under every circumstance. Mastering the basics makes doing advanced techniques much easier. All of Reeders' students worked on the fundamentals. Senior students also went on to more advanced practices.

Reeders was cautious who he taught. A fighting art like kuntao attracted many unsavory characters. In his later years it seems he stopped teaching aspects of kuntao that he valued so much. He must have found it easier to teach the essentials for self-defense and exercise forms that were designed primarily for health benefits.

On the following pages are examples describing fundamental techniques to illustrate the essence of the Reeders' style and his attitude that molded his techniques.

Foot Patterns & Esoteric Floor Diagram

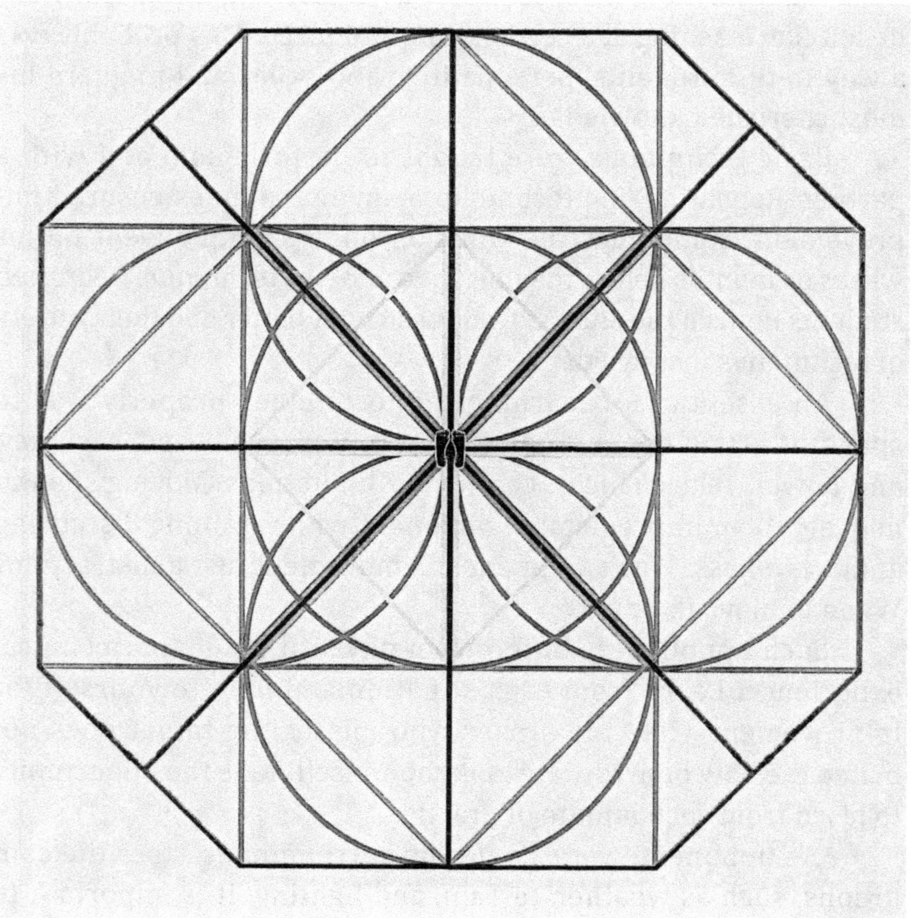

Diagram provide by Robert Servidio.

The above diagram is a helpful reference for understanding how one can move in different directions utilizing foot and body postures that they have learned. Withing the diagram, each geometric figure is usually drawn with a specific color, making it easier to see how they overlap and give a structure to the diagram. A person can imagine standing on specific points on the diagram at any given time in relation to any surrounding (person/s, object/s). An opponent can also be viewed as present on their own pattern.

There are infinite ways to move around the diagram, through triangles, squares, and circles. Moving through the diagram is like discovering the rooms in a building, working in one area to get to know it well, then moving into another area to discover the possibilities.

Usually, one starts by imagining standing in the middle of the diagram, shown by the two feet drawn in the center. Step directly to another point where lines cross. The movement may be straight as in a forward step, or round as in a sweep. Each type of technique performed is practiced for improving stability while recognizing the opponent or multiple opponents in the arena.

On another level, we see an individual placed in the universe. What are the relationships to all outside oneself? How do we relate to all else? This would not only include our positions with opponents, but with other individuals, friends, family members and even plants and planets, and other objects. This is the mystical side of the diagram—a simple diagram that can be studied for a lifetime.

Technical Repertoire

Movements with the feet are connected to whole body. We can think in terms of attacking and defending, but for Reeders often there was no distinction. For example, if someone attacked with a straight, forward punch, his "block" would be directed at the elbow joint to break it. His defensive block was also a crippling attack. For an open hand attack, he may break a finger or dislocate the shoulder. With this approach, it is easy to understand why so much of the Reeders' system could not be used in tournaments.

Going to another level, an attack could be deflected while finger striking to the opponent's throat—both accomplished with one movement of a single arm, not two. Or the opponent's attack could simply be ignored by moving out of its path while a lethal blow is struck to the solar plexus.

For Reeders there were no rules to protect the opponent. As he would say, "We are dirty fighters." The main targets would be chosen for their susceptibility and likelihood to cause death or to be crippling. A strike to the chest was not done to knock someone back, but to stop their heart. Rather than knockout an attacker with a punch to the jaw, a back hand finger strike would be aimed at the trachea to stop their breathing.

The use of the fingers is practical for attacking vital areas, including the eyes and acupoints. Palm strikes are valued for inflicting damage that disperses over a wide area. Think of an arrow (fingertip) penetrating a target verses a sledgehammer (palm) hitting a cement surface. The various hand formations are tools shaped to fit their job. A tiger paw fits the outline of the jaw. A single knuckle penetrates the jugular notch. A palm strike is suitable as a percussive blow.

Just as the hand structure provides so many combat tools and uses, all other body parts are considered in applications. A simple shift of weight can topple an opponent by the hip pushing him off balance. Most martial art practitioners are familiar with how the feet, knees, legs, elbows, arms and shoulders are utilized for blocking, striking, throwing and tripping. The possibilities are endless.

There is an illustration originating from Ernest de Vries that depicts the names of eight styles of kuntao placed on tree branches. While most think an individual would study one of the styles, Reeders would use techniques from all the styles. He absorbed techniques from the systems and used the most appropriate tool for the job.

Accuracy and power of the techniques were essential. Today those sparring in tournaments are using protective gear and their techniques are not very accurate. They rely on the gear for protection, or their attacks may be off the mark while being close enough to get a point. For example, to target an eye or a tiny vital point, a fingertip would be used to precisely hit the mark the size of a dime. In Indonesia, some masters improve their accuracy by striking at tiny objects attached on moving strings.

Also in Indonesia, practice is often done at night, the cooler part of the day in the tropics. Another reason is to become less reliant on one's vision to become more sensitive to the movements made by opponents and the environment. Some practice blind-folded. This type of training is extremely rare. Most in Indonesia in modern times are attracted to taekwondo or modern silat studied for show and performed under bright lights.

Reeders retained many of the older methods himself. You would see the results in the individual techniques and the rou-tines he performed. The attitude and objectives used in the open-hand techniques were the same for any weapon. Sword, knife or staff would be an extension of the open-hand. The body movement adapted to the various weapon designs to be suitable for its qual-ities such as slicing, stabbing, or crushing.

The taichus and staff were two of Reeders favorite weapons. However, anything in his hands was lethal. Master of eighty-eight weapons? Why such a limiting number? A pen, magazine or beer bottle could be an effective weapon too. I wouldn't want to attack Reeders if he had a broomstick in hand.

Conclusion

In this chapter, I have tried to present Reeders' martial system as I've observed over the past sixty years. This is not the Chinese system of Liu Seong because Reeders expanded what he learned from his master, especially with elements from Indonesian silat styles. Thus, we have Reeders' system of "Chinese hands and Indo-nesian feet."

Regardless of style, the individual students of a single master will comprehend and perform differently than their teacher and fellow classmates. Reeders' senior students had different levels of understanding and skills. Some were naturally gifted and learned techniques easily while other struggled. Many remained too hard, in large part from their earlier studies of karate. A few of the first-generation students grasped much of Reeders' system, but not all of it. Some of the second generation reflect Reeders' style very well. Like Humpty Dumpty who had a great fall, nobody could put him together again.

Long ago Richard Lopez predicted that much of the Reeders' system would go to the grave with him. The master's teachings were too much for any single student to absorb. The time and place are very different from days in Java to days in New York or New Mexico.

Photographs and videos cannot convey the mental state and kinetic movement associated with the personal kuntao style Reeders attempted to teach. He went beyond physical technique and styles, grasping the deeper principles of a universal martial art. Although his system is elusive, he inspires many toward the discovery of the richness of what a martial system can contain.

It is a shame that 8mm movie films taken of Reeders on the peninsula of Erie, PA, were stolen from Raymond Cunningham's studio. Perhaps these are lost forever. Even photographs of him are rare. What we have left are many stories and some facts that each now can sift through and interpret to their own understanding who Reeders was as a man and kuntao master.

Reeders forged his spirit and art through the chaotic days in Dutch-Indonesia, working on plantations, fighting against the Japanese, being a prisoner of war and escaping, fighting for the Dutch against the Indonesian independent forces, then struggling as an immigrant in America. Many great martial artists praised Reeders, appreciating his rare skills and abilities. His martial spirit continues today through fine representatives of his system, including second and third generation teachers.

chapter VI

A Memoir of Kuntao Studies

Martial Essence: Pepperman and Sykes

My introduction to the martial arts was accidental. I can't remember the details as to exactly when and where it happened. I do remember that I was attending Sacred Heart Grade School in Erie, PA, transitioning into eighth grade in 1966. The dawn of puberty may have contributed to the foggy memory. At the time, I had some fuzz on my chin and was one of the tallest among classmates. I haven't gotten much taller since. There was some wrestling with the nuns, who would take you by the ear to a bathroom to cut your hair if it was too long. They didn't like my Elvis style, but my dad didn't concur with their wishes. He had the same hair style. I wasn't influenced by Elvis, but nobody could be sheltered from the advent of The Beatles.

Then came weekly guitar lessons. After learning three chords, others appeared having the bright idea that we could play music: Jeff Orlando, Sid Michaels, Luther Gibbs, Eric Johnson. . . But we needed a singer. Someone volunteered a guy named Thomas Pepperman (1951–2013). As we struggled with three-chord progressions, Tom was a natural singer. He knew the lines and hit the notes effortlessly. He had a bluesy voice, close to a Paul Butterfield or Charlie Musslewhite. Along with the rock-and-roll standards, we did play some blues.

The band practiced at the home of Luther's parents, which wasn't in the better part of town. And Tom lived smack dab in one of the rougher areas. It is no little wonder why Tom was studying a martial art. I wasn't comfortable in his neighborhood even during daylight hours. Many parts of the city were unsafe, and I thought it wise to ask Tom if I could also learn self-defense. He took me to meet his teacher, Arthur "Sonny" Sykes (1934–2008). It is only by looking back over the decades that I now see the significance of this as a life-changing event.

Sometimes Sykes stayed in Erie, but he was living in Cleveland at this time. Anytime he came to Erie, we'd workout. I remember the first time going up a couple flights of stairs above a bar in an old building on 6th and French Streets to a studio. Others taught in the space on that floor too, but we'd be there when others were not around. A large painted dragon decorated a wall. The old wooden floors had been sanded smooth and painted grey. Dressing rooms were in the back. Large windows faced the two-block area called Perry Square, named after Admiral Oliver Hazard Perry, famed naval commander during the Battle of 1812 on Lake Erie. Perry's name may be familiar to some for his role in the 1854 Convention of Kanagawa which opened Japan to the West.

Over the months, it was usually only Sykes, Tom and me meeting together to work out. Sykes would show us techniques. Tom and I would repeat and repeat a new single technique for hours and regularly review over following months. He was more advanced than his brown belt indicated. Working with him certainly nurtured my practice. Often, I'd work on individual techniques while he practiced a solo barehanded routine or with weapons. We varied our practices according to Sykes guidance. Many days just Tom and I worked out, reviewing lessons and sparring.

The techniques Sykes was teaching focused on evasive shifting and stepping in unison with various combinations of blocking, deflecting, and striking. We'd move according to imaginary geometric patterns on the floor based on a triangle, usually standing on one point and moving to the other two, or standing on two points and stepping to the third. One triangle could be attached to another, so the foot patterns could get complex. With enough triangles, circles could be formed. In normal practice, we didn't think much about this. We just moved.

Of course, stepping patterns worked in tandem with the whole body to perform any strike, kick, reap, throw, or break. Mainly closed-hand techniques would be used in tournaments, but much of the system called for open-hand techniques useful for grabs, strikes to the most vulnerable areas (eyes, throat and groin), and to vital points. Hand formations became tools, for example: a claw shape suitable to grasp an opponent's jawbone, a single knuckle that fits into the jugular notch, or using the index finger for eye strikes while the other fingers serve to prevent too deep a penetration by coming against the cheekbone. Each movement was executed for maximum effect. Rather than simply block an incoming punch, a block/strike could be utilized to break the elbow. Rather than sweep a leg, the knee was destroyed. Sykes' teacher, Willem Reeders, was quoted as saying: "We are dirty fighters." Many of the individual techniques were embodied in solo routines. Training always allotted time for sparring.

Later, I discovered that this wasn't how other martial art instructors taught. They usually had schools occupied with a dozen or more students. The only reason why we practiced this way—basically private lessons—was because Tom was like an adopted son for Sykes. Sykes had dated Tom's mother and they remained good friends. Affection would show in small ways, Sykes always called him "Tommy," even though Tom was a few years older than I and a senior attending Academy High School. Little Tommy had grown up.

I can't remember when the building on French Street was torn down and became the location of Erie Insurance Corporate Headquarters. We moved over to another old building called Pythian Temple at 524 West 17th Street. This was once a building for the fraternal organization known as The Knights of Pythias. For us, the second floor served well for our practice with a huge area. Its wooden floor was maintained well, since we always sparred barefoot. I remember seeing it darken by spots of sweat from our workouts. At this location, new students joined and classes became larger. More students for practicing techniques in pairs and for sparring.

The new students presented different characters. Most were good classmates, but sometimes there would be a troublemaker. Now with the larger classes, there was much activity. I was working individual techniques while a few others were sparring. One big guy who was sparring started yelling at his opponent in a blood rage. Sykes quickly moved toward them and, speaking is a soft voice, cooled down the heated conflict. He managed to keep a wonderful atmosphere in classes, with an emphasis on respect. Rarely would

Friend and teacher, Thomas Pepperman, here rarely without a smile.

anyone get hurt, even during the most intense sparring sessions, in large part because control and accuracy were emphasized for any and every technique.

When I was promoted from white belt to green, Tom gifted a belt to me which was originally give to him by Sykes, and to Sykes from his teacher, Willem Reeders. I didn't think much about belts. I was just happy learning and enjoying our friendships. Tom was promoted to orange sash and was fighting in the black belt category at tournaments. I spent much time with Tom in and out of the *dojo* — a Japanese term most Americans used for the practice hall. Many called our art "karate," but we knew it as Royal Kung Fu. It took me a few more years to comprehend the full significance of the name.

The art took time to learn as did the history and who was involved in its development and transmission. The main figure was Grandmaster Willem Reeders, who I was told was of royal Chinese and Dutch heritage. He came to the USA from Indonesia. I met him and many of his senior students, including Richard Lopez, Raymond Cunningham, Guy Savelli, Patrick Sheldon, and others. During my high school years, I'd go to tournaments in Pennsylvania and neighboring states, representing Sykes' school. Many other teachers and styles would be present, mainly Okinawan karate stylists.

In the late 1960s and early 1970s, most Americans were only familiar with karate and judo. The "little dragon," Bruce Lee, had not yet entered the scene. Tournament judges favored their own styles, so it wasn't easy to win trophies if you were a Royal Kung Fu practitioner. The judges didn't understand our techniques, which often appeared softer than karate. For example, a karate practitioner would strongly block a kick at their head, fiercely pushing the attacking foot far offline. For the same type of attack, we'd shift away and deflect with one hand brought up near the ear. The kicking foot may be close to our head, but it was as good as a mile away. There is no need to over-extend such a block, which then offers an additional target for your opponent. It took many more years for judges to learn about the logic of Chinese styles and how they worked.

Besides the bias of style, Sykes was a black man, a very black one! There was prejudice against him and his students because of this. He was also an extremely good martial artist, and jealousy filled the room when he'd walk into a tournament. Once I was sitting in the bleachers waiting for a tournament to begin. Schools were arriving by busloads. One well known high-ranking instructor stopped

Michael DeMarco, Tom Pepperman, Jeff Orlando & David Lewis.

in front of me to ask another instructor: "Is Sykes here?" If Sykes was present and entered in the tournament, experienced black belts knew they would have a very difficult fight for a first-place trophy.

Those entering tournaments could participant in different categories, usually being forms, sparring, and breaking. For forms, each performer would announce their personal name, style, school, and the name of the routine they intended to demonstrate. I've seen Sykes enter the black belt division doing forms I never saw previously. He could jump into the air with a silken sidekick that struck out and returned like lightning. Accurate to their targets, his hand strikes were blurs of color. If there was a tie for first place, the referees would ask the two participants to perform again. Sykes would usually announce the name of a different form to perform. Later I learned he just spontaneously improvised forms. It is difficult enough to practice a form thousands of times and later perform it well in front of judges. Although he did memorize and teach many routines, Sykes could create a form on the spot. It'd be flawless. Try to move through a few seconds of improvised techniques at fighting speed and discover the difficulty. To this day, I don't know anyone else who can do this.

Sykes and Tom always did well in the fighting division. What was fascinating to me was that most of what we practiced in the studio could not be used in tournament fighting. Trophies were won with points. The Reeders' system was for real fighting, not competition. The techniques were to cripple or maim, so we limited and adapted for tournaments.

Sykes was caring for all his students. At tournaments, he'd closely watch the fighting bouts for fairness and safety. I never saw him angry. He'd face problems calmly as he would while competing on the floor. During the years I studied with him, he treated me as family, with kindness, patience, and understanding. The first time he gave me a ride to my parents he met my father. "Hey Dad! Look who I brought home!" It was a rare occurrence to see a white man, and a charcoal-black man greet and shake hands in a middle-class milky neighborhood during the early 70s, the time following the Watts riots in Los Angeles. This is a great memory for me because the two men were similar in many ways. A bow for their ability to have sympathy for everyone.

My father, Ralph DeMarco, never studied martial arts, although he was a superb athlete in many sports. Tom was at my parents' home one day and we were talking about breaking methods. Tom showed me how to break a red brick. Not any easy feat. If attempted with poor technique, it is an excellent way to break one's finger bones or wrist. My father watched us, walked over, kneeled, and broke a brick on his first try. I'm glad my dad never spanked me during my youth.

As mentioned, I had some difficult classmates, and Sykes did too. At the start of our workout at the Pythian Temple on a particular day, one of Reeders' students came in wearing a red sash. Standing in the middle of the big room, he challenged Sykes. Our teacher walked slowly out from the dressing room and sat on a chair facing the floor. Why was the challenge made? I am unsure of all the details, but it seems there was a question of the authenticity of the high rank shown by the red sash. Sykes didn't go on the floor, but softly spoke until the unwelcomed guest left, the intruder promising to the settle the matter at another time and place. Looking back on this strange episode, Sykes did not accept the challenge because he knew the only end would be with someone severely wounded or perhaps even in a death. He didn't need to prove anything in that way.

Months later, Tom and I went to meet Sykes at the Pythian Temple to practice. It was out of the ordinary that more than a dozen black belt holders were also arriving. Sykes arranged a few long tables for them to sit and talk in the side room while Tom and I practiced in the main room. The meeting was to discuss what they could do about this challenger. How to prove he did nor did not deserve and receive a red sash? The black belts were of various styles, and the question of rank was difficult for them to solve in this case. Their meeting had no results.

By the early 1970s, Sykes was unable to come to Erie so often. Tom and I looked for a school, mainly for practice space. We went to a few schools, including Vincent Christiano's and Gerald Durant's Goshin Jutsu karate dojos. Christiano was a good fighter. One of his favored techniques was to jump high into the air to come down upon you with an overhead strike (*shuto*). It was 95% successful because he was a large man, falling on you like a tidal wave. The shuto was only the coup de grâce. We also attended Durant's classes. I enjoyed working with one of his top black belt students and gentleman, Steve Capella. Durant registered me in Japan as a purple belt. But Tom and I were already infused with Royal Kung Fu and we didn't stay very long at the school.

At one tournament, off to the side, Durant was demonstrating with Japanese *sai* (a short metal weapon with two prongs) techniques to Reeders and others. Reeders was watching, standing motionless in his typical mode, with his arms hanging down, hands crossed in front. As the sais glistened through the air flipping and spinning, Reeders suddenly plucked both sais away with one hand while they were in movement. Reeders style was not so flashy. All his techniques—open hand and with weapons—focused on the practical. Tom was becoming quite familiar using the sais and knives. I hadn't started any weapons work as yet.

Shifu Richard Lopez with the author.

Tom opened his own school on Eleventh and State Streets. At least a few hundred people attended the grand opening. Tom was getting many students, no doubt in large part due to Bruce Lee's raising star. Much changed. I loved Royal Kung Fu but didn't want to spend time with some of the new students. As with Reeders' following and Sykes' following, Tom was getting some problem students. To keep a distance from those I felt were of low character, I decided to sacrifice studies. I didn't know if I would ever study with anyone else again.

Five Quarters for a Dollar: Richard Lopez

Some months passed. I went to a car wash and needed four quarters for a dollar to start the machine. I asked a guy in the next stall if he had change. He said he recognized me from the black belt meeting at the Pythian Temple. His name was Richard Lopez (1933–2014), another student of Willem Reeders. After learning that I stopped studying under Sykes and Pepperman, he invited me to where he was teaching. It was in a studio behind the home of another Willem Reeders' student named Raymond Cunningham (1928–2008), located at 439 East 6th Street. Ray was a tough ex-Marine with good, often salty, humor. He had a nice small studio behind his house. Although Cunningham, Sykes, and Lopez had the same teacher, there were differences in how they moved individually. Both Cunningham and Lopez utilized more tension in their movement than Sykes, but they had an excellent repertoire of techniques and knew how to use them. Both had studied karate and judo previously which probably influenced their gongfu. Cunningham's skills were tested on his job. He worked twenty-six years as a detective for Norfolk and Southern Railroad where he thwarted several would-be train robberies.

The 6th Street studio remains vivid in my mind. In the winter, I'd arrive early to shovel a path through the snow down the long driveway leading to it. There was a small office on the left of the entry with a smaller bathroom/dressing room. The workout area was not large. Only two people could spar at a time. Two photos of Reeders were on one wall, and one of judo founder Jigoro Kano. At center was set of *taichu* (jp. *sai*) mounted in a triangular shaped board. Judo matts were rolled up and kept along the same wall. A long closet contained many judo uniforms. Only eight to a dozen students were in a class, usually working techniques in pairs. No real sparring. We did practice some throws and falls. A benefit was that Lopez did start me with basic weapons practice: taichu, knives, staff, and broadsword.

Lopez loved working with weapons and made many. He made personalized sets of taichu for Reeders according to specifications Reeders set down. I've held a heavy set made for practice, seemingly designed for weightlifters. Of course, others made for regular usage would then seem relatively light. Even the regular sais were substantial, making the store-bought models feel like toys. In Japanese, *sai* (釵) means "hairpin" because of its shape. It is called "iron ruler" (*tie chi* 鐵尺) in Chinese, *tekpi* in Malay; *chabang* or *tjabang* in Indonesian, and *tepi* in the Hakka language that Reeders spoke. Reeders usually called them "hairpin" or *taichu* in Hakka. Reeders explained to Lopez that the taichu's length should properly match the length of the practitioner's forearm. The distance between the main section and the prongs were measured by finger-widths so as not to be too tight or too loose for maneuvering.

Time moved on. While living twenty miles away on the campus of Edinboro University (now called PennWest), I'd get to Lopez's class once a week. Some of the usual practitioners there included Mark Anthony, Joe Sanfratello, Ron Cargioli, Peter Pjecha, and Jerry Hayes. Good memories of the studio and the after-class shrimp and a beer at the Friendly's Tavern on West 8th and Chestnut Street.

When Lopez purchased a house at 1012 West 27th Street, he converted a two-car garage behind the home to include a second-

Willem Reeders & the author in Jamestown.

floor studio. Some students continued at this location and new students joined classes, including Charles Page, Tony Flagella, Michael Marchini, Ed Brooks, and Al Mele. A few helped in the studio's construction. I painted a four-by-eight-foot dragon for the wall. Unlike regular dragon designs, this one had five talons, a symbol of royalty. Other instructors would sometime visit the Lopez studio, especially local karateka such as Billy Blanks, Ralph Porfilio, and Artis Simmons.

While home from college for the weekend, Lopez called to invite me out for a for Chinese dinner at the Inn of Double Happiness on Peach and Liberty Streets. When I arrived at the restaurant, he was sitting at a big table with his wife Alice and a few others. It was on this night that he presented me with an orange sash—equivalent to a black belt. I was his only orange sash. I appreciated it, but I never wore it. Thinking of all the familiar schools, I had seen so many undeserved black belts that I questioned the real value of rank. Plus there were others of great talent who weren't promoted. Lopez would periodically tell me to wear the belt. Eventually he gave up talking about it. Even later, he stopped wearing his third-degree orange sash. Knowledge was more important than the belt. However, forty years later I told Lopez I should have worn it just because it was from him.

As part of my undergraduate work, I went to study philosophy in India in 1974 at Vivekananda College, affiliated with the University of Madras. That brought an end to my regular studies with Lopez. However, we remained in close touch for the next forty years. He became like a father, and we met often as close friends.

Considering the length of time studying at the 6th Street and 27th Street studios, I didn't make much progress in martial skill. I would eventually go to Taiwan to study. At that time Lopez said he didn't have anything more to teach me. He had years of experience in judo, karate, and the Reeders system. He had more cards up his sleeve but didn't feel they would add to my deck. What he shared were personal stories of his martial art studies, including his knowledge of Willem Reeders and the Royal Kung Fu system.

During those more than forty years with Lopez, he shared much with me. I learned it was he who found and remodeled the studio on 6th and French. He talked of the tournaments and all of Reeders' students. He often talked with great respect about Robert Servidio, who he eventually introduced to me. Servidio is perhaps the most knowledgeable about Reeders' system. Like the Grandmaster, Servidio has a triad on his hand, three small dots tattooed on his purlicue—the space between the thumb and the forefinger. The dots have a special significance for Reeders and the martial system.

Note: This chapter is an edited extract from: DeMarco, M. (2023).

Photographic Record

Three photos on Erie beach showing Reeders flanked by Raymond Cunningham on the left and Robert Servidio on the right. Courtesy of Richard Lopez.

Above: Group photo, kneeling left to right: Servidio, Reeders and Cunningham.
Below: Two other photos courtesy of Thomas Pepperman.

Above: Willem Reeders at center with Robert Servidio on the far right.
Below: Reeders closely observing practice. Servidio on the right.

Above: Scott Young, Servidio and Reeders. Below: Reeders with finger strike toward Gerald Durant. Four photos courtesy of R. Servidio.

World Kung-Fu Federation

Certificate

This is to Certify that

Art Sykes

has been thoroughly trained in KUNG-FU, the deadly art of self-defense. Physically and mentally tested, and satisfactorily passed all the requirements set by the Chung Hwah Kung-Fu Hui: for the rank

of **orange** sash. **Hon'ary 4th degree**

Vice President, TAN KIM SJONG, Hong Kong

Chairman, PAUL TJAN, Toronto-Canada

Advisor, SAM WONG, Toronto-Canada

President-Chief Instructor

Willem A. Reeders

7th Dan Red Sash

6-20-70

Certificate presented to Arthur Sykes by Willem Reeders (signatures, including "Liu Seong" in Chinese). Courtesy of Joe Salomone.

Above photo courtesy of Joe Salomone; below courtesy of Thomas Pepperman.

Richard Lopez

Three photos of the author
studying with Richard Lopez.

Below, two photos practicing
with fellow classmate
Ronald Cargioli.

All photos by M. DeMarco.

Appendix: Coming to Terms

When Willem Reeders started teaching in the United States, most Americans had only heard of karate and judo as martial arts. Reeders and other teachers of non-Japanese styles would often resort to using the term "karate" instead of the unfamiliar and foreign sounding styles, such as taijiquan, gongfu, and kuntao. It took many years for the vocabulary to become more familiar. Over fifty years have passed and the terminology is still confusing with many people misusing important words. Examples are too numerous to list, but some idea is illustrated in the paragraphs below.

Decades ago, one of Willem Reeders' senior students gave a presentation at the grand opening of his own student's new martial art school. Each word in his short speech captivated the audience. He praised his student's accomplishments in the Reeders' system and for the accepting the responsibility for transmitting the art. Attempting to tie ancient Chinese combative traditions to a praise-worthy philosophy, the name of Confucius was invoked. The name Confucius was Latinized by the Jesuits for Western readers. Looking in reference books of the day, the Chinese characters were pronounced as *Kong fuzi*. Members of the audience understood the significance as how China's great sage had ties to Chinese martial arts, "kungfu." *Kong* (孔) is the sage's surname. In Japanese, it is pronounced as *Kung*. *Fuzi* (夫子) signifies "master." Kungfuzi or Master Kungfu = Confucius. However, the characters for the martial term *kungfu* (功夫) are different with a totally different meaning (hard work requiring time). Even the romanization of this term has since changed and is now usually written as *gongfu*.

Without an agreement on the meaning of key martial terms, it is impossible to have a meaningful discussion or use the terms in a publication. There are many barriers with the first being cultural. Evening after years of studying Chinese, a native English speaker will make mistakes in understanding and translating. For example, a literal translation of *xianren zhi lu* (仙人指路) would be "immortal finger way," but *zhi* (finger) here infers "to point": the immortal points the way.

Many learn the meaning of a Chinese character, such as *qi* (氣) meaning vital life force or energy. So, anytime they hear the sound "qi" they think they know what the word means. There are four basic tones in Mandarin for characters. Every single sound would fall under a tone and may have ten or more meanings for each tone. One sound pronounced with one tone may have ten different characters and their own unique meanings. So, one sound pronounced with different tones could easily have ten to fifty meanings. One character added to another, and their combination quickly multiplies the number of possible meanings. *Dong* (東) means east. *Xi* (西) means west. *Dongxi* (東西) means "things"—the items you may find in between cardinal points.

We have another obstacle in our quest to understand Chinese words. If you see a Chinese character for the first time, how would you pronounce it? An English speaker has absolutely no clue. Scholars developed systems so non-Chinese could learn the language, including speaking, hearing, and writing. The earliest systematic Romanization of Chinese began with Jesuit missionaries in the 16th century. A few hundred years later, another system was developed called the Wade-Giles system. The Hanyu Pinyin system was developed on mainland China in 1958 and is the most common system used today.

Taoism is not pronounced as it looks because according in Wade-Giles the "t" is pronounced as a "d". Today you find the word spelled as Daoism in Hanyu Pinyin. The "t'" in *t'ai chi* is pronounced as a "t" because it has an apostrophe after it. Without the apostrophe it would be pronounced as a "d." In Hanyu Pinyin it is Romanized as *taiji*. I remember a university professor lecturing about "Tay-o-ism" . . . His area of specialization was not China and can be forgiven for this common mistake.

Confusing enough? . . . Yet there is more. One top of the complexities of written Chinese and the Romanization systems, there are hundreds of distinct regional dialects. The surname 譚 can be pronounced *Tan, Tam, Tom or Hom*, depending on the dialect. Reeders spoke a dialect found in southern China and its diaspora called *Hakka*.

Some say Willem Reeders' uncle was surnamed Liu (劉), which is pronounced as Lau in Cantonese. Liu and Lau are not different names but are different pronunciations. There is also confusion about the uncle's familiar name, with some arguing over the change of spelling: Siong, Cong, Seong, etc. Again, the character remains the same with only the Romanization being different. Nobody should argue over Romanization.

Another major source for debate is the term *kuntao*, which is also Romanized as *kuntaw*. This term has no special attachment to Willem Reeders' fighting system. Anybody can use the term. It is simply a word denoting a martial art. It is different from *gongfu* (*kungfu*) in literal translation, but *gongfu* is often used to signify martial art because learning a martial art takes so much time and effort to learn. Kuntao and *quan dao* have similarities with another Chinese martial term, *quanfa* (拳法), *quan* meaning fist or boxing and *fa* meaning method or law. These terms are as interchangeable as *martial art*, *combat art*, and *fighting art*.

Reeders also studied *silat*, another general term used for the martial arts found in the Malay Archipelago. Styles of Southeast Asian silat number in the hundreds.

Martial art teachers should take their work seriously enough to invest some time in learning the basic foreign terms used in their style. Students benefit from this too. Below are a few terms commonly used by practitioners of Reeders' system.

Chinese Glossary

Wade Giles	Pinyin	Character	
ch'üan	quan	拳	fist or boxing
chuanfa	quanfa	拳法	boxing method
kungfu	gongfu	功夫	work and time (to obtain skills)
ch'üan tao	quan dao	拳道	boxing way (*kuntao/kuntau*, Hakka)
tao	dao	道	the way, path, or road
t'ieh chi	tie chi	鐵尺	iron ruler

Regardless of what culture is being referenced, many refer to the Japanese *sai* when talking about this weapon. Reeders used the term *taichu* (Hakka); 簪子 (characters); *zanzi* (Mandarin); meaning "hairpin." Another character for hairpin is 釵, pronounced *chai*. Also known as *chabang* (Indonesian); *tjabang* (Dutch); and *tekpi* (Malay).

Scholarly References

ALEXANDER, H., CHAMBERS, Q., AND DRAEGER, D. (1974). *Pentjak-silat: The Indonesian fighting art.* Tokyo: Kodansha International Ltd.

CHAMBERS, Q., AND DRAEGER, D. (1979). *Javanese silat: The fighting art of Perisai Diri.* Tokyo: Kodansha International Ltd.

CLAVER, A. (2014). *Dutch commerce and Chinese merchants in Java colonial relationships in trade and finance, 1800–1942.* Leiden; Boston: Brill.

CORDES, H. (1990). Pencak silat: Die kampfkunst der Minangkabau und ihr kulturelles umfeld. Ph.D. dissertation, University of Cologne, Germany.

DAVIES, P. (2015). What is kuntao? Cultural marginality in the Indo-Malay martial arts tradition. In Davies, et. al., *Indo-Malay Martial Traditions: Aesthetics, Mysticism and Combatives, Vol. 1.* p. 1–22.

DEMARCO, M. (2023). *The Best Fight: a memoir of a martial art practitioner, publisher, and author.* Santa Fe, NM: Via Media Publishing.

DEMARCO, M. (2015). Practical fighting strategies of Indonesian kuntao-silat in the Willem Reeders tradition. In Pauka, et. al., *Indo-Malay Martial Traditions: Aesthetics, Mysticism and Combatives, Vol. 2.* p. 73–90.

DOHRENWEND, R. (2002). *The odd East Asian sai. Journal of Asian Martial Arts, 11*(3), 8–29.

DRAEGER, D. (1972). *The weapons and fighting arts of Indonesia.* Rutland, VT: Tuttle Publishing.

DRAEGER, D., AND SMITH, R. (1969). *Comprehensive Asian fighting arts.* New York: Kodansha America.

FARRER, D. (2009). *Shadows of the prophet: Martial arts and Sufi mysticism.* Berlin, Germany: Springer.

HELLWIG, T. (Ed.), Tagliacozzo, E. (Ed.) (2009). *The Indonesia reader: History, culture, politics.* Durham, NC: Duke University Press.

IZZAH, L., SULISTIYONO, S.T., AND ROCHWULANINGSIH, Y. BONDOWOSO (2019). In the encirclement of private plantation companies in the colonial era. Proceedings of the 1st International Conference on Environment and Sustainability Issues, ICESI 2019, 18–19 July 2019, Semarang, Central Java, Indonesia.

IZZAH, L., SULISTIYONO, S.T., AND ROCHWULANINGSHI, Y. (2020). David Birnie: A Dutch private investor and agent of social change for society at Bondowoso East Java, Indonesia in the colonial era. IOP Conference Series: Earth and Environmental Science. 485.

Kroese, C.E. (Summer-Autumn, 1973). Dutch trade with the People's Republic of China. *Law and Contemporary Problems* Vol. 38, No. 2, Trade with China, pp. 230–239.

Maliszewski, M. (1992). Meditative-religious traditions of fighting arts and martial ways. *Journal of Asian Martial Arts, 1*(3), 1–104. See subheading on "Indonesia," pages 26–29.

Maliszewski, M. (1990). Personal videotape recordings taken through Asia, including Indonesia.

McKissick, R., Parker, D., with Rooney, A. (2019). *The Liu Seong kuntao broken mirror system.* Santa Fe, NM: Via Media Publishing.

Nasution (June 2011). Economic development of colonial Surabaya and its impact on natives, 1830–1930. *Historia: International Journal of History Education*, Vol. XII, No. 1.

Palmier, L. (1965). *Indonesia and the Dutch.* London: Oxford University Press.

Parker, C. (2015). Opening and closing: An introduction to the welcoming postures of pencak silat. In Pauka, et. al., *Indo-Malay Martial Traditions: Aesthetics, Mysticism and Combatives, Vol. 2.* p. 91–106.

Pauka, K. (2015a). The Pauleh Tinggi ceremony in West Sumatra: Martial arts, magic, and male bonding. In Davies, et. al., *Indo-Malay Martial Traditions: Aesthetics, Mysticism and Combatives, Vol. 1.* p. 74–94.

Pauka, K. (2015b). Silek: The martial arts of the Minangkabau in West Sumatra. In Pauka, et. al., *Indo-Malay Martial Traditions: Aesthetics, Mysticism and Combatives, Vol. 2.* p. 1–24.

Pauka, K. (2015c). A flower of martial arts: The Randai folk theatre of the Minangkabau in West Sumatra. In Pauka, et. al., *Indo-Malay Martial Traditions: Aesthetics, Mysticism and Combatives, Vol. 2.* p. 25–44.

Pauka, K. (2015d). Silat-based Randai Theater of West Sumatra makes its U.S. debut. In Pauka, et. al., *Indo-Malay Martial Traditions: Aesthetics, Mysticism and Combatives, Vol. 2.* p. 45–59.

Pauka, K. (1999). Randai and silek: Folk theatre and martial arts of the Minangkabau in West Sumatra. CD-ROM. University of Michigan Press.

PAUKA, K. (1998). *Theater and martial arts in West Sumatra: Randai and silek of the Minangkabau*. Athens, Ohio: Ohio University Press.

RICKLEFS, M. (1993). *A history of modern Indonesia since c. 1300*, 2nd edition. Stanford: Stanford University Press.

TOER, PRAMOEDYA (2008). *The Chinese in Indonesia*. Madison, Wisconsin: Select Publishing.

WILEY, M. (2015A). Silat kebatinan as an expression of mysticism and martial culture in Southeast Asia. In Davies, et. al., *Indo-Malay Martial Traditions: Aesthetics, Mysticism and Combatives, Vol. 1*. p. 63–73.

WILEY, M. (2015B). Silat Seni Gayong: Seven levels of defense. *Indo-Malay Martial Traditions: Aesthetics, Mysticism and Combatives, Vol. 2*. p. 60–72.

WILSON, J. (2015). Chasing the magic: Mysticism and the martial arts on the island of Java. In Davies, et. al., *Indo-Malay Martial Traditions: Aesthetics, Mysticism and Combatives, Vol. 1*. p. 23–62.

Popular References

ARMY, M. (June 1, 1986). Master of ancient discipline retains youthful vigor. *Albuquerque Journal*, p. 8, Section D.

BURDICK, J. (August 9, 2023). Artis Simmons and the endless road: Erie's "Gem City Ace" dominated the martial arts circuit with an impeccable sense of cool. Erie, PA: Erie Reader. www.eriereader.com/article/artis-simmons-and-the-endless-road

HINES, J. (1964). *Action for Men*, "The rampage of the red ant: Fantastic saboteur who held off a Jap division," p. 12–13.

LANIOUS, E. (n.d.). A conversation with Gary Galvin.

McGAN, P. (April 28, 1970). Karate masters among visitors here to honor Willem Reeders. *Evening Observer*, Dukirk Fredenia, N.Y.

REYNGOUDT, G. (2006). Willem Reeders: An unofficial biography. Self-published.

Ancestry Websites

Ancestry	www.ancestry.com
National Archives, The Hague	www.nationaalarchief.nl
Genealogy Online	www.genealogieonline.nl
CBG Center for Family History	https://cbg.nl
Wie Was Wie (Who Was Who)	www.wiewaswie.nl

Indo-Malay Martial Traditions

Aesthetics, Mysticism & Combatives Volumes I & II

VOLUME ONE

➡ **What is Kuntao? Cultural Marginality in the Indo-Malay Martial Arts Tradition**
Philip H.J. Davies, Ph.D.

➡ **Chasing the Magic: Mysticism and the Martial Arts on the Island of Java**
James Wilson, J.D., Dip. Ac./Lic. Ac.

➡ **Silat Kebatinan as an Expression of Mysticism & Martial Culture in Southeast Asia**
Mark V. Wiley, B.A.

➡ **The Pauleh Tinggi Ceremony in West Sumatra: Martial Arts, Magic & Male Bonding**
Kirstin Pauka, Ph.D.

VOLUME TWO

➡ **Silek: The Martial Arts of the Minangkabau in West Sumatra**
Kirstin Pauka, Ph.D.

➡ **A Flower of Martial Arts: The Randai Folk Theatre of the Minangkabau in W. Sumatra**
Kirstin Pauka, Ph.D.

➡ **Silat-Based Randai Theater of West Sumatra Makes its U.S. Debut**
Kirstin Pauka, Ph.D.

➡ **Silat Seni Gayong: Seven Levels of Defense**
Mark V. Wiley, B.A.

➡ **Practical Fighting Strategies of Indonesian Kuntao-Silat in the Willem Reeders Tradition**
Michael A. DeMarco, M.A.

➡ **Opening and Closing: An Introduction to the Welcoming Postures of Pencak Silat**
Chris Parker, B.Ed.

The Liu Seong Kuntao

Broken Mirror System

by Reginald Mckissick
and Dexter Parker
with Alejandro Rooney

CONTENTS

- **Chapter 1: Background**
  History, Basic Concepts and Philosophy, Preservation versus Modernization,
  Characteristics of Liu Seong Kuntao, Attitude and Mindset
- **Chapter 2: Stances and Footwork**
  Fundamental Concepts, Stances, Footwork, Training
- **Chapter 3: Hands and Arms**
  Blocking and Parrying, Closed-Hand Strikes,
  Open-Hand Strikes, Elbow Strikes, Training
- **Chapter 4: Legs and Knees**
  Kicks, Foot Sweeps, Defensive Countermeasures Against High Kicks, Training
- **Chapter 5: Flow**
- **Chapter 6: Forms**
  The Southern Set, The Leopard Set, The Low Tiger Set
- **Chapter 7: Qigong**
  Basic Relaxation Techniques
- **Chapter 8: Putting It All Together**
- **Lineage Chart and Bibliogreaphy**

Alejandro Rooney assembled this book through research and interviews with Grandmaster Reginald McKissick and Master Dexter Parker. The result is a detailed overview that includes the historical background and the theory and practice of Liu Seong's art, reflecting like a "broken mirror" all of the arts embodied in the martial system.